THE COMPLETE HANDBOOK OF CLOCK MANAGEMENT

REVISED 2009

Homer Smith

COACHES CHOICE

©2009 Coaches Choice. Revised edition. All rights reserved. Printed in the United States.

No part of this book may be reproduced, stored in a retrieval system or transmitted in any form or by any means, electronic, mechanical, photocopying, recording or otherwise, without the written permission of Coaches Choice.

ISBN: 978-1-60679-028-1
Library of Congress Control Number: 2008943226
Book layout and diagrams: Deborah Oldenburg
Cover design: Jennifer Bokelmann
Front cover photo: Jeff Gross/Getty Images

Coaches Choice
PO Box 1828
Monterey, CA 93942
www.coacheschoice.com

Dedication

Dedicated to the quarterbacks with whom I worked, under the clock.

Dick Norman, Stanford

Terry Isaacson, Air Force Academy

Tim Murphy, Air Force Academy

Jimmy Poole, Davidson

Gordon Slade, Davidson

John Read, UOP

Carlos Brown, UOP

Mark Harmon, UCLA

Rob Scribner, UCLA

John Schiarra, UCLA

Scott Gillogly, Army

Leamon Hall, Army

Earl Mulrane, Army

Jay Schroeder, UCLA

Tom Ramsey, UCLA

Rick Neuheisel, UCLA

Steve Bono, UCLA

David Norrie, UCLA

Matt Stevens, UCLA

Brendan McCracken, UCLA

Bill Kenney, K.C. Chiefs

Todd Blackledge, K.C. Chiefs

David Smith, Alabama

Gary Hollingsworth, Alabama

Jim Bonds, UCLA

Tommy Maddox, UCLA

Rob Walker, UCLA

John Barnes, UCLA

Wayne Cook, UCLA

Brian Burgdorf, Alabama

Jay Barker, Alabama

Freddie Kitchens, Alabama

Keith Smith, Arizona

Brady Batten, Arizona

Ortege Jenkins, Arizona

Acknowledgments

My appreciation to the head coaches for whom
I played and worked is inexpressible.

The late Charlie Caldwell at Princeton, my coach,
made me want to be a coach.

The late Jack Curtice at Stanford, an offensive pioneer,
encouraged my first writing efforts.

Ben Martin at the Air Force Academy, an exemplar,
demonstrated how to bring out the power in young people.

Pepper Rodgers at UCLA, brilliant and daring, sold me on systematic football.

Terry Donahue at UCLA, wise and thorough,
let me do crazy things to make crucial points.

Frank Gansz at the Kansas City Chiefs, a former military pilot,
showed me what preparation for fail-safe performance means.

Bill Curry at Alabama, a 10-year NFL center, had answers for my questions.

Dick Tomey at Arizona, a winner, gave me my final chance
to get clock management right.

Special thanks to veteran SEC referee Al Ford for listening
and advising, and to University of Georgia coach,
Mark Richt for a stimulating exchange.

Extra special thanks to my wife Kathy
who typed football materials for 46 years.

Contents

Dedication 3
Acknowledgments 4

Chapter 1: Introducing the Challenge 7

Chapter 2: Figuring Time 14

Chapter 3: Playing Fast 22

Chapter 4: Assembling Weapons 30

Chapter 5: Using the Intentional Incomplete Pass, The Spike ... 47

Chapter 6: Using Time-Outs 53

Chapter 7: Distinguishing between Procedures and Decisions ... 59

Chapter 8: Clarifying Objectives 63

Chapter 9: Squeezing in Next-to-the-Last Plays 70

Chapter 10: Using Up Excess Time Before Scoring 76

Chapter 11: Letting Your Opponent Score a TD 81

Chapter 12: Using Clock Offense in a Wind 86

Chapter 13: Deciding on Kicking a FG or Going for a TD 91

Chapter 14: Deciding on Punting or Going for a First Down ... 97

Chapter 15: Deciding on an Extra Point in Final Seconds 102

Chapter 16: Trying for Two Points 105

Chapter 17: Taking a Safety 111

Chapter 18: Keeping the Clock Moving. 122

Chapter 19: Preparing the Quarterback. 130

Chapter 20: Practicing. 138

Chapter 21: Playing Clock Defense 148

Chapter 22: Sustaining Progress 152

Appendices 156

About the Author. 175

1

Introducing the Challenge

Facing the Responsibility

The playing of football is at its best when players accept responsibility for the playing. When one player blames one coach for one problem, the playing is not at its best.

The managing of the clock is at its best when coaches accept responsibility for the managing. When one coach blames one player for one problem, the managing is not at its best.

Preparing for the playing is year-around and is supported by staffs and facilities. Preparing for the managing should be year-around and be supported by whatever will help. This book is to help.

Needing a System

You need a system for dealing with a moving clock, multiple variables, necessary barriers, ever-changing relativities, and demanded decisions. You need a system with structures, reference points, procedures, and warnings. You need a system for thinking ahead.

> ***You cannot escape clock management,
> not when there is a scoreboard clock.***

A system has answers. Systematic clock management, like systematic theology, covers everything that can happen. This book describes a system.

Recognizing the Difficulty

You have to plan forward on a clock that moves backward. You have to think ahead in numbers that require subtraction. You have to do arithmetic when numbers will not stand still.

Before a play you have to know the possible plays to call after the play. Before the play there may be five possible best-calls for five possible situations after the play, depending on the possible results and on what the clock might be doing.

Each of three variables—time, points, and ball-position—affects the effect of each of the other two.

Each of these familiar tactics can be wrong:

- throwing for a sideline,
- spiking to stop the clock,
- getting out-of-bounds to stop the clock,
- saving a time-out for a field goal, or
- taking a knee to consume remaining seconds.

After a game your critics may take two days to figure out what you should have done. You may have had two seconds.

Case: Louisville is going to beat Florida State. On the field, it is "clock city." In the final two minutes the TV commentators cover: a statue of Johnny Unitas, the Louisville QB having met Unitas, FSU's sack history, the weather, the FSU aura that is not there, the field's ability to take rain, Michael Jordan returning to the NBA, the defensive player of the game, and what went on earlier. Few things are more difficult than thinking ahead in a football game when the clock is involved, and the commentators avoided doing it.

> *A system, by definition, covers everything and has answers. You need a system.*

Imagining Situations

Imagine yourself in situations that suggest the subjects of the 22 chapters:

- You want to improve your clock offense. Where do you start? Is there a right approach? What are you in for? Chapter 1 INTRODUCING THE CHALLENGE

- You are on his 12 in the second quarter, with one time-out and 00:36 on a first-down clock. What can you get done? Chapter 2 FIGURING TIME

- Needing 10 points to win, you are on his 42, with the clock stopped at 02:19 for a measurement. It will be 2nd-and-inches or 1st-and-10. What should your team be doing during the measurement? Chapter 3 PLAYING FAST

- You have to go 63 yards in 01:23 to get the winning touchdown. You have two time-outs. Is there a formation that will facilitate playing fast? Chapter 4 ASSEMBLING WEAPONS

- You need either a field goal or a touchdown in the 2nd quarter. It is 2nd down on his 23, with 00:19, 00:18 showing on a moving clock as your first-down play ends. Your time-outs are gone. Should you spike and kick? Or, should you call an end-zone-pass/spike package and let your QB spike only if he sees at least 00:03? Chapter 5 USING THE INTENTIONAL INCOMPLETE PASS, THE SPIKE

- Your opponent is going to be punting to you from his 18 if he fails to make a first down. You have one time-out and 02:19. You need a field goal to win. Should you use your last time-out on his punt or save it to use on your offense? Chapter 6 USING TIME-OUTS

- You find yourself hesitating when decisions seem equally right and wrong. How can you keep from doing this? Chapter 7 DISTINGUISHING BETWEEN PROCEDURES AND DECISIONS

- Before halftime you are on your 41, with two time-outs and 01:13. How many yards do you need to average per play to get a touchdown? Chapter 8 CLARIFYING OBJECTIVES

- You need a field goal to win. Your time-outs are gone. It is 2nd-and-10 on your opponent's 28, with 00:39, 00:38 on a moving clock. You need six yards to get to the field-goal line. Can you get six, but not a first down and, then, spike to get the clock stopped? Or, do you have to go for a boundary or the first-down line? Chapter 9 SQUEEZING IN NEXT-TO-THE-LAST PLAYS

- You are on your opponent's 14, with two time-outs. It is 3rd-and-five, with 02:48, 02:47 in the second quarter. You do not want to leave him any more time than you have to. Should you run and consume 40 seconds, or should you pass with a slightly better chance to get a 1st-and-goal but with a 50-percent chance of an incomplete consuming only five seconds? Chapter 10 USING UP EXCESS TIME BEFORE SCORING

- With 01:37 remaining and the score tied, your opponent has a 1st-and-goal on your five. Not having a time-out, should you let him score and count on driving and answering with seven points and getting into overtime? Chapter 11 LETTING YOUR OPPONENT SCORE A TD

> ***No coach can work alone and prepare himself for managing the clock.***

- Near a change of quarters, the wind is against you. It is 3rd-and-nine, with 00:11 showing. You want to pass because the chance of making nine with a pass is better than it would be with a run; however, an incomplete would leave you against the wind, and even if you run, your opponent may use a time-out and keep the wind. What should you do? Chapter 12 USING CLOCK OFFENSE IN A WIND

- In the fourth quarter you are ahead by three, with 01:01 and 4th-and-goal on the four. Your opponent has two time-outs. Do you try to score a TD and go ahead by 10 but risk leaving him behind by three with 55 seconds and a chance to drive, kick, and tie? Or, do you kick and force him to drive all the way for a touchdown to win? Chapter 13 DECIDING ON KICKING A FG OR GOING FOR A TD

- Behind by five in the fourth quarter, you have 4th-and-10 on your 36, with one time-out and 02:52, 02:51. Should you punt and count on giving your opponent no more than three plays and getting the ball back with time to score? Or should you go for the 10 yards and, if you fail, count on stopping him in four plays and getting the ball back where it is? Chapter 14 DECIDING ON PUNTING OR GOING FOR A FIRST DOWN

- You just scored with 10 seconds left in the game, to go ahead by two. Do you kick the extra point to protect yourself against his answering? Or do you take a knee so he cannot block your kick, scoop it up, and score two points to tie you? Chapter 15 DECIDING ON AN EXTRA POINT IN FINAL SECONDS

- You have just scored to get within five, 20-25. It is the middle of the third quarter. Should you go for two? Chapter 16 TRYING FOR TWO POINTS

- It is 4th-and-12 on your one-yard line. You are ahead by three. The clock shows 05:01, 05:00, and your opponent has three time-outs. You are worried about a blocked punt. Should you take a safety? Chapter 17 TAKING A SAFETY

- You need to get rid of 01:21, 01:20, or you will have to punt from around your 42. It is 3rd-and-six. The clock is moving. Your opponent is out of time-outs. Do you run or pass? Chapter 18 KEEPING THE CLOCK MOVING

- Playing without a time-out, you have called for a first-down pass, hoping to get to the field-goal line with time to spike. Just beyond the field-goal line your QB sees 00:02 on a first-down clock. What must you have prepared him to do? Chapter 19 PREPARING THE QUARTERBACK

- You are going for a winning FG, without a time-out, and you must get to your opponent's 22. It is 2nd-and-10 on his 28, with 00:33 showing on a stopped clock. What should you do? Chapter 20 PRACTICING

- Your opponent is behind by two and has 2nd-and-10 on the 50, with 00:59 and no time-outs. He passes. Your pass defender intercepts. What should he do? Chapter 21 PLAYING CLOCK DEFENSE

- You are wondering how you can practice all of this thinking-ahead. Chapter 22 SUSTAINING PROGRESS

> ***Players play the game. Coaches manage the clock.***

Anticipating the Presentation

I address "you". You are the decision-maker. You are never the quarterback or a sideline clock-management specialist. Mostly, you are the head coach. Sometimes, you are a pressbox play-caller. "He" is the opponent decision-maker.

The clock times given are the times that show as plays end. These are the times you take mental snapshots of before making decisions. Time on a moving clock is represented by two times, like 00:21, 00:20.

Special words help, such as:

- time-out run, for a run that will stop the clock by use of a time-out
- white cap, for the ref, who is the official the QB can get answers from
- ref's time, for the time the ref takes to allow for substitutions and start the 25-second counter
- answer, for the score that is needed because of a score
- first-down clock, for the clock that is stopped by a first down but stopped only until the ball is declared ready for play
- change-of-possession clock, for the clock that will stay stopped until the 1st-down ball is snapped

Case: Army, losing to Louisville, finds itself on the Louisville 31, with two time-outs and 00:19. A run-oriented team with a back who had on that day set a school record for rushing yardage in a game, Army throws three passes, incomplete, and misses a 48-yard FG. They could have had two time-out runs in place of two of those passes. Apparently, they associated 00:19 with a need to pass. Apparently, they did not associate time-outs with opportunities to run.

The real-game cases, from televised games, reveal what can happen when the clock becomes a factor. Some cases include botched commentary by otherwise sharp football men who are identified only as the "booth". The numbers and quotes are from notes taken from personal video tapings from 1999 through 2002. I include these cases to make the point that clock management is very, very difficult. Without them, the point would not be sufficiently made. The perpetrators are schools and booths, not individuals; except for one—the author.

A first down is what you make. The 1st down is the first of the four downs.

Your half of the field is the minus half; his, the plus. You might punt the ball from the -30 to the +30, or, from your 30 to his 30.

I use my own numbers: e.g., five seconds for a play if you are trying to keep the clock moving but 10 for a play if you are trying to keep it stopping. If your numbers are different, you can plug them in without affecting the advocated system of clock management.

Only quinary numbers are used in initial considerations of time. Why? Because no numbers would be the right ones, and 5s are easier to deal with than 6s and 7s. (A flustered person is said to be "at all 6s and 7s".) Because it is better to begin with simple numbers and then fudge beyond them. Because fudging allows coaches and QBs from different levels of experience to begin with the same simple numbers.

I assume play-calling from a pressbox. Only from above can a distance-to-go be known as soon as a ballcarrier goes down; only by knowing that distance quickly can a call be made quickly.

As of 2008, when an official signals that the ball is dead, the play clock shall begin a 40-second count. If an official signals for the game clock to be stopped for any of the following reasons—any time-out or administration, a penalty, a measurement, a change of possession, after a kick down, a score, a start of a period, or an instant replay review—the clock is to be set at 25 seconds. Potential time consumption, then, is essentially the same as it was in 2007. I figure it to be 35 seconds.

I assume that final control will be by the QB on the field. Only the QB can:

- see the clock and either the 25-second or the 40-second counter in its relationship to the snap count,
- ask when a stopped clock will start,
- hear penalty choices, and
- talk to the ref.

Enclosed tables are for laminated sideline cards, cards that a clock-management specialist needs in order to bring all preparation to the game field. Every coach has what he calls a card for two-point play decisions. It is wise to have cards for other decisions.

Chapters separate clock problems. They vary in length because problems vary in explicability.

> **Clock times that show as plays end are the times upon which decisions are based.**

2

Figuring Time

Clock managing is seeing the time remaining on the clock when a play ends and doing whatever you need to do. Clock managing begins with knowing how the clock works and how much time things take.

Understanding the Clock

Any official signals that the clock is to be kept running by winding one arm and that it is to be stopped by crossing both arms over his head. The referee signals that the 25-second counter is to start by dropping one hand sharply and tooting his whistle loudly.

> *Reputation, leadership, intelligence, investment, will power, momentum—none of these make any difference to the clock.*

The clock will stop and stay stopped until the snap if it was stopped for:

- a time-out,
- an incomplete pass,
- an out-of-bounds ball within the last two minutes of each half

- a penalty on a side that the ref believes took the penalty to consume time, which means that (a) the defense cannot jump offsides and give up five yards in order to consume the seconds that it would take for the offense to initiate a play after the ball is declared ready and (b) the offense cannot take a delay penalty, absorb the five-yard loss, and get the clock moving again without executing a play,
- something that interrupts the 25-second counter.

The clock will start with the ref's hand-signal and toot if it was stopped for:
- a first down,
- a penalty, except when taken to consume time,
- an injury,
- a measurement,
- an out-of-bounds ball outside of the last two minutes of each half,
- a TV time-out,
- game administration
- a forward fumble out-of-bounds, on the principle that you cannot take a five-yard penalty to get the clock stopped until the snap,

As of 2007, the clock will start on a free kick when the ball is legally touched on the field of play and will stop when the ball is declared dead.

It should go without saying that a player cannot affect the clock by faking an injury, faking an equipment problem, calling for a measurement, or complaining.

The QB must know, positively, when a stopped clock will start. He can ask the ref, and he should get a quick answer—"on the snap" or "on the ready". A coach cannot ask.

Case: Virginia, losing, runs out of seconds before running out of downs on the Colorado State three. Actually, they lost a fumble but, if they had not, they would have just barely run out of seconds. Could they have saved some time on a drive that began on their 17? Yes. Especially when there was a measurement at 01:15 and they did not snap the ball until 01:01. Unwisely, they did not stay on the line during the measurement.

Case: Northwestern needs two TDs against Minnesota, with 01:44 left in the game. Someone in the stands blows a whistle, and a Northwestern play disintegrates at 01:40. The ref gives them back the play. The coach stops the game and makes him give them back the four seconds, too. Northwestern scores. Minnesota fouls. Northwestern kicks off from the 50. The intentionally short kickoff goes to the five. Minnesota runs three plays and punts. Northwestern moves and, at 00:03, spikes the ball. A Hail Mary wins it. Credit the Northwestern coach who insisted on his four seconds.

If a pass is completed on a sideline near the first-down line, there is a chance for confusion. If the QB sees an official cross his arms over his head, he does not know whether it is to stop the clock until the snap or until the ready signal. That official's procedure, when the ball is inbounds for a first down, should be to wind one arm and then cross both arms. If the first signal may have been missed, the QB must ask, "When will the clock start?

> **The QB must know, positively, when a stopped clock will start. He can ask the ref, "When will the clock start?"**

After a play ends, there is another chance for confusion. If an official just crosses his arms and stops the clock, you may not know what it is for—TV time-out, defensive time-out, game administration—and, if you do not know for sure when the clock will start, your QB must ask.

> **Neither side can intentionally give up a 5-yard penalty and control the clock. The Ref is allowed whatever discretion he needs to deny this.**

As for the matter of trying to use up time by taking penalties, here is an example of what the defense *could try to do*:

The offense has 1st-and-10, with 00:13. The ball is declared ready. The clock starts. The defense jumps offsides at 00:10, just as the QB starts his cadence. The clock stops. The defense is penalized. It becomes 1st-and-five. The ball is declared ready. The clock starts. The offense is slow in getting lined up. The defense jumps again, at 00:05. The clock stops. The defense is penalized. It is still 1st-and-10, but eight seconds are gone, and the offense has one play left instead of two.

Obviously, this practice is unacceptable—trading yards for the consuming of time. The ref is given the discretion he needs to deny it.

Here is an example of what an offense *can do*:

The offense has 1st-and-10, with 00:41. The clock starts. The offense lets the 25-second counter run out and takes a delay penalty. The ref does not start the clock on the ready signal, but it is still 1st down. The offense runs its 1st down play normally, and it becomes 2nd down. Again, the 25-second counter is allowed to run out, and five yards is stepped off. The clock does not start, but it is still 2nd down.

Understanding Time Consumption in Real Time

In real time, which is wristwatch time, how do you estimate how long things will take? It depends on whether you are trying to save time so something can happen or trying to spend time so something cannot happen. If you are trying to save, you want to be high in your estimates; if you are trying to spend, you want to be low.

> ***If you are trying to save time, you want estimates of consumption to be high.***

Estimated consumption in real seconds is

- for a play—10 or 5,
- for the ref—15 or 10,
- for the 25-second counter—20,
- for the 40-second counter—35,
- for a spike—2,
- for taking a knee or falling on the ball—2,
- for keeping the ball alive—5, and
- for a hurry-on of FG or punting personnel and a kick—20.

If you are trying to stop the clock or squeeze in a next-to-the-last play or punt before a change of quarters or score after you have given up a safety or if you are doing anything where you feel short of time, you want to be high—10 for a play and 15 for the ref. If you are trying to bleed the clock or punt after the change of quarters or keep your opponent from scoring after you have given up a safety or if you are trying to do anything where you have more time than you want, you want to be low—5 for a play and 10 for the ref.

The consumption for a spike is estimated to be two seconds, which is high; for taking a knee, two seconds, which is low. The consumption for keeping the ball alive is estimated to be five seconds, which is low; for hurrying field-goal or punting personnel on and kicking, 20 seconds, which is high.

Again, if you are worried about not having enough time, you want to be high so you will not find yourself without time that you were counting on having. If you are worried about having too much time, you want to be low so you will not find yourself with time that you thought you were going to be rid of.

If you are playing fast and have estimated high, a 7-second play and a 13-second ref will *not* surprise you; if you are playing slow and have estimated low, the same 7-second play and 13-second ref will *not* surprise you.

> *If you are trying to spend time, you want estimates of consumption to be low.*

Can you affect the length of time that the ref takes to declare the ball ready? He would say, no, but it certainly seems that either hustling or not hustling and either creating piles or avoiding creating them can affect the length.

Varying Speeds of Play

Your speeds of play are in real time. Logical separations are:

- Fast
- Hustle
- Normal
- Deliberate
- Slow

FAST is as fast as the ref will let you play, with an average of about 5 seconds for a play and about 15 seconds to get the ball ready—20 seconds of real time per play. (This includes only one of the conservative estimates—the 15 for the ref. It does not include the other conservative estimate—spare 10 for a play.)

HUSTLE is with no wasted motion and with about 20 seconds left on the 25-second or the 40-second counter—25 seconds per.

NORMAL is with normal substituting, huddling, motioning, and checking and with 5 seconds for a play, 15 for the substitution, and about 15 left on the counter—35 per.

> *20 seconds per play is about as fast as the ref will let you play.*

DELIBERATE is slow but with 10 offensive players not knowing that it is slow, with liberal substituting, long motioning, slow checking, and 5 seconds left on the counter—40 seconds per.

SLOW is with wide inbounds running, creative piling, reluctant unpiling, general dragging of the feet, and 2 seconds left on the counter—45 seconds per.

Case: Florida State needs a FG to beat Miami. It is 27-29. After an FSU 1st-down play at the edge of field-goal range, Miami takes a time-out at 00:21. "That's good thinking" comes from the booth. But they give FSU a play to get closer, when they are going to win by a missed FG by a right-footed kicker from the right hashmark, not by a long drive in 15 seconds after the FG. FSU runs left with a 2nd down, spikes, kicks, and misses. Could they have played faster and saved enough time for a 3rd-down run in place of the spike? Yes. (1) They wasted a time-out earlier. (2) They lost 15 and 19 seconds after first downs. They actually huddled. (3) The QB got tackled at 01:29, and a time-out was not called until 01:23. Enough time.

Case: Army, down by 10 to Navy with a first down on Navy's 48 at 02:36, gets the ball snapped at 02:13. That is 22 seconds wasted. Army, with another first down at 01:52, gets the ball snapped at 01:38. That is 13 seconds wasted. At 01:13 they get a field goal and are down by seven. An onside kick fails but, if it had succeeded, how much would they have wished they had played faster?

Adjusting Time Consumption for Clock Time

In clock times, how long do things take? Clock times are real times minus the times when the clock is stopped. It can be stopped between plays or between a play and the ready signal. Let us separate time-conserving efforts from time-consuming efforts.

Estimated consumption for clock-stopping next-to-the-last plays when you are conserving is, for a play initiated

- out of a stopped clock, 10 seconds,
- out of a temporarily-stopped clock, 15 seconds (allowing 5 between the ball-ready signal and the snap, and 10 for the play),
- out of a moving clock, 30 seconds (allowing 15 for the substitution, 5 between the ball-ready signal and the snap, and 10 for the play).

Estimated consumption in clock seconds when you are consuming time is, for a clock-stopping play initiated

- out of a stopped clock, 5 seconds,
- out of a temporarily-stopped clock, 25 seconds (allowing 20 from the 25-second counter and 5 for the play),
- out of a moving clock, 40 seconds (taking only one of the two time-consuming estimates, for either the ref or the play—e.g., 15 for the ref, 20 from the counter, and 5 for the play).

In clock times those are the numbers with which you can deal.

> **The clock may be stopped during the ref's time or during the ref's time plus the 25-second-counter time.**

Choosing a play is a problem when you are conserving, because your first choice for the down-and-distance may threaten to consume too much time, and you may have to go to your second choice or to your third.

Figuring consumption of clock time is critical when you must protect the initiating of a last play while trying to squeeze in a next-to-a-last play. For a given situation, you must know, precisely, the consumption times of the plays you are considering. Final plays, of course, require only the one second that it takes to initiate them.

Anticipating Clock-Time Consumptions

Variations in consumption of clock time are extreme. Only extensive practice in simulations can keep you from being surprised. Examples:

- With a 1st-and-goal and a stopped clock

    00:05 means one run or one end-zone pass,

    00:10 can mean either one run or an end-zone pass and, then, either a run or a pass,

    00:15 can mean either one run or two end-zone passes and, then, either a run or a pass,

    00:20 can mean either one run or three end-zone passes and, then, either a run or a pass

    00:25 can mean either two runs or three end-zone passes and, then, either a run or a pass,

    00:45 can mean either three runs or any combination of runs and passes and, then, either a run or a pass,

    01:05 can mean either four runs or any combination.

- From the +12, a TD pass can take four seconds. From there, four slow plays getting a 1st-and-goal and four more getting a TD can take one-third of a quarter.
- A time-out called on your stop-the-clock offense can save you 15 seconds and add three plays. A time-out called on your opponent's move-the-clock offense can save you 45 seconds and add 6 or 7 plays.
- After a change of possession, four knee plays, for which your opponent has three time-outs, can take 8 seconds. After a first down is made, four ball-alive plays and no opponent time-outs can take 150 seconds.

- Generally, in a given amount of time and completing 50 percent of your passes, you can execute about twice as many passes as you can runs.
- You can execute almost as many plays making first downs as you can getting the ball out-of-bounds.
- A pass that sends a receiver out-of-bounds may take five seconds; one that keeps him in for less than a first down can take 40.

> ***It is possible to consume extra time while making the rhythm at the line seem the same.***

Incidentally, the time-of-possession statistic that is given with other offensive statistics is meaningless.

3

Playing Fast

Considering a Way to Do It

This is a way:

- The QB acts simultaneously with the ending of a play and either calls a time-out or signals for the clock-offense formation, left or right. If he signals, he looks to the sideline as he does.

- The distance-to-go assistant, in the pressbox, has the first-down line visualized in relation to the closest yard line. With the ending of the play, he sees where the linesman puts his forward foot, which is the farthest point that the forward tip of the ball has reached.

- The assistant's arms are already circled around the play-caller's head. From the visualized first-down line, the linesman's foot, and the yard line, he figures the distance-to-go and shows it with his fingers, instantly.

- The play-caller can see the fingers without looking directly at them. He has a play ready for each distance and for a first down, and he calls one.

- The sideline signaler gets the call and raises its one-handed signal over his head.

- The QB, before even thinking about what is being signaled, duplicates the signal with a raised hand.

> **Play is the fastest if the play-caller is in the pressbox.
> There, with help, he can get a new distance-to-go immediately.**

- The other 10 players had started for their positions with the signaling of the formation, and they see the QB's signal as soon as it goes up.

- The called-play has a specified player who points to his assignment. The other players assign themselves off of the point. If secondary communicating is needed—this would be by two or three blockers who see their two or three targets but must divvy them up—it is done verbally.

- Either the tee QB or the shotgun center waits for the ref's whistle toot and gets the ball snapped.

When the clock is moving or is stopped for a first down, this is a way to play FAST. It should produce a play in every 20 seconds of real time.

Only if it is certain that a stopped-clock will stay stopped until the snap, can there be a substitution or a huddle. A coach who tries to send in a play to a huddle, when there is a first down and the clock stops only temporarily, almost always costs his team a play in the drive. If there is to be a substitution or a huddle or a different formation when the clock stops for an out-of-bounds ball or an incomplete pass, the clock personnel and formation must be restored automatically the first time there is no out-of-bounds or incomplete. The players who do the restoring get the play-signal on the run, and the QB makes no allowance for the traffic.

Case: Just before halftime, Fresno State tries a FG from the Wisconsin 39, on a 2nd down, and misses. What kept them from being able to use their 2nd and 3rd downs to get closer? Six things: (1) The QB runs out-of-bounds to stop the clock when he could have gotten a first down and done the same. (2) Coaches lose 13 seconds on a measurement. (3) A receiver fails to get out-of-bounds, short of the first-down line, when he could have. (4) A time-out is called after a first down is made, after the clock has stopped. (5) Same. (6) With 1st-and-20 on the Wisconsin 31, with a time-out and 00:28, only one play is executed before the kick. It is difficult to keep abreast of clock considerations, and during the drive the booth discusses (a) whether a sacker should be allowed to land on a passer, (b) the weight the Wisconsin coach has lost, (c) a player being from the West Indies, and (d) a past BCS selection.

Huddling

In FAST play, if the clock stops on an out-of-bounds or an incomplete, should you huddle? Yes and no.

- Yes, if you want (a) to change either personnel or the formation or (b) to call a play for which there is no signal.
- Yes, as long as the QB will be able to return smoothly to whatever he needs for FAST play.
- No, if it is more important to keep the defense from huddling and substituting.
- No, if it is more effective to keep the QB in FAST play, with no change in rhythm.

Case: Clemson scores to go up by four over Georgia Tech, with 2:00 left. Tech takes the ball on its own 20, with three time-outs. They will score and win. How? (1) They lose no time getting the ball snapped after first downs. (2) They use their time-outs to add plays. (3) The clock never runs between plays. (4) They get off 14 plays for 80 yards in one minute and 53 seconds. Now, that is two-minute offense!

Maintaining the Speed

If there is a measurement, a penalty, or an injury, the ball can be snapped just after the ready signal. If the yardage is short or if the ball must go to the end zone, the rhythm can stay the same. This is because every kind of play, from a QB sneak to a Hail Mary, can be executed without a formation change or a substitution. Excepting the play-callers part, none of this is difficult.

> ***With trim and rhythmic communications plus some hustle, a play can be executed every 20 seconds.***

The play-caller must decide on possible next plays right after the calling of a play. The possible next plays must be laid out mentally in the 15 seconds between finishing the verbalizing of the call and having to begin the verbalizing of the next call. While he is deciding, a play is actually being communicated and executed. A QB, who is at the line and must change a play, has no time at all to think. He must be able to go, by rule, from one kind of play to another.

Case: Iowa State wants to beat Florida State and has two minutes, three time-outs, and the ball on their own 25. The game will end, for them, with 1st-and-goal on the one-yard line, with 00:04. Could they have saved some time on their 74-yard drive? If they can just execute a play every 20 seconds, lose no more than one second after getting a first down, and call time-out immediately after a play ends, they can have 27 more seconds with that 1st-and-goal.

Playing Fast, by Players Other than the QB

Everyone must

- know how to read the QB's hand-signals,
- know how to run to his position and land with his feet in place,
- know how to have his feet set before the ball is spotted and to be motionless in his stance before the ref toots his whistle,
- know how to derive assignments from individuals who point to their targets,
- know how to play in noise without verbal communication, with only hand-signaling and pointing,
- on measurements, penalties, injuries, and any game administration, know how to get lined up and be ready for a quick snap-signal and, on measurements and penalties if the ball is to be moved, how to take a check-off,
- know how to participate in a hurry-on of field-goal personnel.

> *A coach who tries to send in a play for a 1st down, because the clock is stopped temporarily, almost always costs his team a play in the drive.*

Linemen and tight ends must

- know how to take over on their designated plays and point to their targets, exaggeratedly, so the other players can derive their assignments.

The center must

- on a shotgun snap, know how to ensure that the QB is looking at the ball, to hear the toot, and to snap immediately.

Receivers and running backs must

- know how to stay inbounds and get out-of-bounds,
- know how to take a pass route beyond the first-down line or the goal line,

- on a next-to-last play, know how to get to the ground before time expires so a time-out can be called.

    Case: Princeton, down 13-14 to Yale, has the ball on its own 20, with 01:12 left in the game and no time-outs. They will score and win, 19-14. The key play in their drive was a boundary pass to the fullback. When he got to the sideline and had the stopping of the clock ensured, he just ran down the line for 44 more yards.

Snapping Fast

In order to snap without losing more than one second, the dropping of the ref's hand must be seen or the tooting of his whistle must be heard.

- In a tee the QB and center must be set, and the QB must either see or hear and then bark a first-sound snapping-signal.
- In a shotgun, the center must be set; he must know his blocking target and be looking back at the QB; then, he must hear, raise his head, and snap.

Case: Penn State is trying to get Coach Joe Paterno his 323rd win to tie the all-time record. With 01:44 left, they are behind Northwestern by four. They are at midfield. They proceed to run plays at 01:44, 01:39, 01:25, 01:15, 01:11, 01:04, 00:54, 00:49, 00:39, 00:33, and 00:25, score, and win 38-35. A share of the all-time record came with one of the all-time clock drives.

Syllogistically speaking, plays are precious; seconds are plays; therefore, seconds are precious.

Doing Nine Things to Play Fast

One, having the play-caller situated in the pressbox where he can get the distance-to-go immediately and accurately.

Two, having a basic formation that can be directed left or right by a one-arm signal and having plays, patterns, and a protection that can be called by one-hand signals and be directed according to the direction of the formation.

Three, having a way to vary the formation without varying either its personnel or the way its direction, left or right, calls for the directions of plays, patterns, and a protection.

> *The ref prevents you from playing as fast as you could possibly play.*

Four, unless the clock is stopped until the snap, doing no substituting except by WRs who must be able to relieve teammates who have just sprinted deep.

Five, having one-hand hand-signals by which plays can be sent to the field, hand-signals that can be copied immediately by the QB and read immediately by the other 10 players.

Six, having blocking assignments that can be derived from specified blockers pointing to their targets.

Seven, having a way to get the ball snapped one second after the ref's toot.

Eight, having special passes that leave

- no chance of a completion inbounds,
- no chance of a completion for less than a first down or a touchdown,
- no chance of a sack, a holding penalty, or an interception.

Nine, having the personnel, the formation, and the plays selected and practiced so they can be used in short yardage and on the goal line.

> **Case:** Florida, admittedly, wants stop-the-clock offense to feel like no more than a hurried version of normal offense. They do not try to play as fast as they could play. Against Tennessee, behind by three in the fourth quarter, they take over on their nine, with 02:14, and get a TD from the Tennessee three, with 00:20. They used two time-outs along the way. They were smooth, but they wasted seconds on every play that did not stop the clock until the snap. The booth: "They don't need a touchdown." Of course, they were going straight for a touchdown and would have kicked only if they had stalled. Coaches usually go for the goal line first when they are behind by three.

Staying Fast through Temporarily-Stopped Clocks

Measurements, penalties, injuries, and game administration, although they stop the clock temporarily, give you extended real time between plays. The first two of those can, however, result in constricted real time between the establishing of the down-and-distance and the declaring of the ball-ready. The result can be fewer than the 15 seconds that the play-caller usually has. (The ref can consume some of them.) A good procedure is to signal for and have ready the play that you want if the chains or the ball are *not* to be moved; and, to instantly signal for and have the QB instantly check to what you want if the chains or the ball are to be moved.

Case: Pittsburgh is behind Iowa State 7-27 and has 3rd-and-2 on the ISU six, with 00:02 left in the half. Did they play fast enough? Looking back, they are on their 25, with 03:13. Wisely, they play normally. They go into ISU territory with 01:18 and, unwisely, they do not play fast. After their first down on the ISU 49, they waste 15 seconds; after they get penalized, they waste 15 more.

Injuries are different from measurements and penalties in that the down-and-distance does not change. They can distract and constrict, however, like any game administration. Change of possession does not constrict. In TV games, following a commercial time-out, the play clock is limited to 15 seconds.

It is possible to execute out of one formation every pass and run that you need for stop-the-clock offense.

Practicing the 20-Second Rhythm

Go through these steps:

1. Get in the clock formation one way, left or right, and execute the same play every 20 seconds.
2. Do this gaining 10 yards each time, without chains, without first downs.
3. Do this gaining 40 yards each time.
4. Repeat step one, alternating between left and right formations.
5. Change the play with every three or four snaps.
6. Still with one alternating formation and a repeated play, introduce first downs and get the ball snapped immediately after the toot of the ref's whistle.
7. Introduce injury time-outs.
8. Introduce measurements and penalties.

All additions are to fit into the 20-second rhythm.

9. Begin signaling in plays from the sideline, limiting the number to three or four.
10. Begin calling plays from the pressbox.
11. Make it gamelike.

Case: Florida State is behind Miami in the second quarter. They have a first down on the +24, with one time-out and 02:16. FSU does not huddle but maintains their normal pace. This loses time after every first down—11 seconds one time, five another, nine another. With 1st-and-goal on the five, the booth says they "may spike it", like they can afford to waste a down with 00:35 showing. With 3rd-and-goal on the two and 00:13, they use their time-out. The booth says they don't have enough time to run and then spike. Spike? On 4th down? Pressure! They have to pass. They cannot run and get off two plays. They do pass, and it is picked. How much must they have wished that they had played faster and saved enough seconds for two runs from the two?

Case: Florida State makes a FG in the second quarter against Louisville. The down was 2nd, the LOS was the two, the time was 00:02. Could they have saved time and been able to use all four downs? Here is where time was lost after they took Louisville's punt at 01:59: (1.) Between the first and second plays of the drive, they use 31 seconds. (2.) After a first down stops the clock at 01:20, they do not snap the ball until 01:13. (3.) Between 1st- and 2nd-down plays, they use 30 seconds. (4.) After a piling-on penalty stops the clock at 00:26, they do not snap the ball until 00:14. That is a cumulative waste of about 37 seconds. They go on to lose the game.

Choosing Not to Signal Plays

National Hall of Fame coach Terry Donahue, when he was at UCLA, had no sideline signaling. Why? He did not want his players coming out of the final game against USC saying, "They've got our signals." Whether USC had the signals or not, his players just thinking that they might have them would have, Coach Donahue thought, taken something away from intensity and confidence. Clock-offense signals had to be excepted.

> *It is possible to play without verbalizing, with only hand-signaling of plays and pointing to targets.*

4

Assembling Weapons

Using One Formation

In order to execute a play every 20 seconds, you need to stay with one personnel unit and one formation, changing only the formation's direction, left and right. Its direction can call the directions of plays, pass patterns, and a pass protection.

The formation shown in Diagram 4-1 is suited for FAST play. It can have a tee or a shotgun QB.

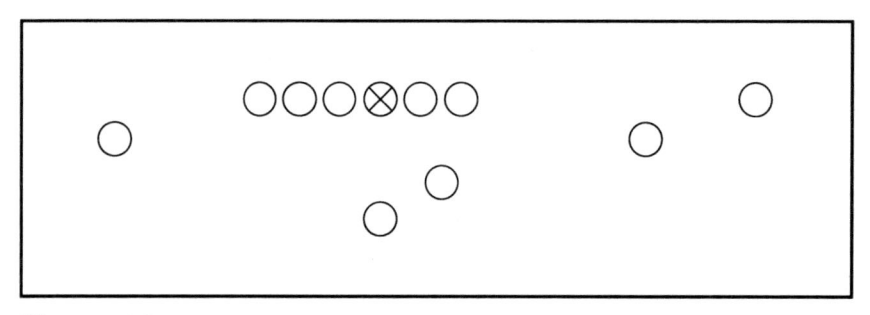

Diagram 4-1

It has 16 features. These suggest considerations for the selection of any basic clock formation.

1. Although balanced, with five and one-half players on each side of the centerline, it has distinctive sides. This increases the types of plays that it can present to a given defense as it is directed left and right. Suggested plays are,

    - to the slotted side, the called side,

        a sprintout run-or-pass,

        a bootleg run-or-pass,

        a QB draw,

        a counter off-tackle run (a.k.a. a counter trey),

        a dropback protection, and

        dropback patterns, and

    - to the tight-end side, away from the called side,

        an inside hand-off run,

        an outside hand-off run,

        an option, out of the tee,

        a QB sneak, out of the tee, and

        a middle trap.

    Weapons should be from what the players know best.

2. Four LOS receivers make it possible to control two safeties and force both corners into single-coverage.

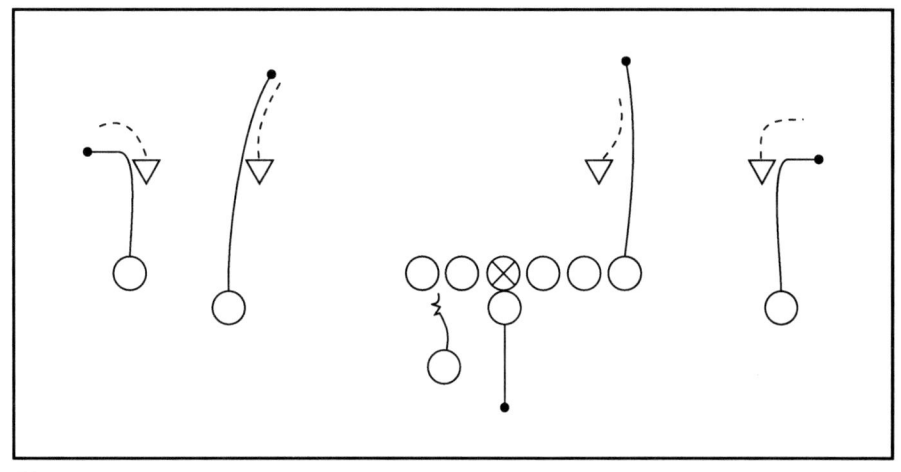

Diagram 4-2

3. The inside LOS receivers and the offset RB make it possible to "stretch" two safeties (with three on two) as long as hitching WRs can occupy the corners. The idea is that the three deep receivers can run beyond the linebackers and that the passer can rifle balls to them.

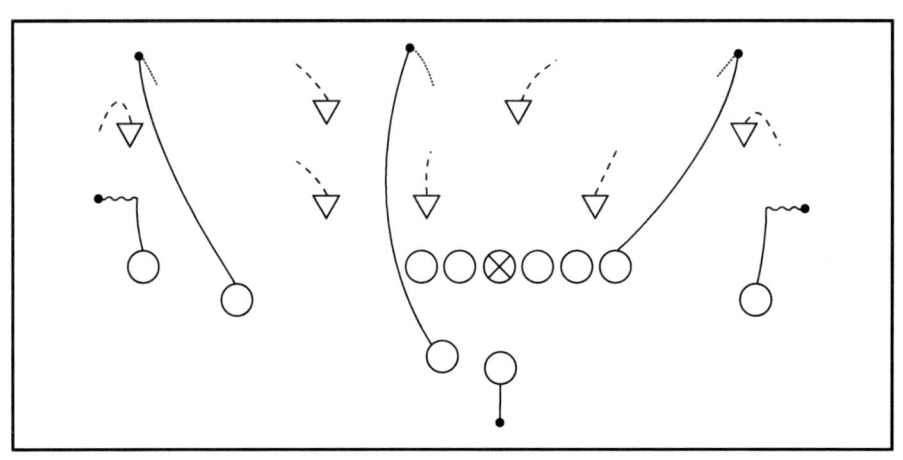

Diagram 4-3

4. A WR on each side leaves open the possibility of WRs not having to cross the field to get lined up when the play is FAST and the direction of the formation is changed. This feature requires only that the WRs learn both sides of WR assignments.

5. Twin receivers, playing about six yards apart, can (a) cross and both go deep on fade, corner, and post routes, (b) cross and one stop and slide either way and one go deep, (c) cross and both go the same way at different levels, and (d) cross twice. The diagram shows them crossing twice. Two physical receivers can just about force the play of three pass defenders on them, which occupies the defender who might otherwise blitz the passer unblocked.

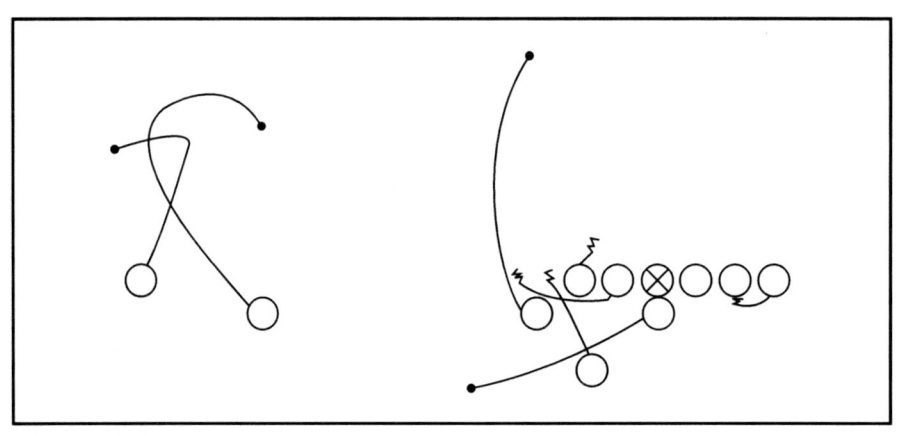

Diagram 4-4

6. The flankerback and the slotback can each create another formation without affecting (a) the relationships of the eight frontal players, (b) the direction of the formation call relative to the RB and TE, or (c) the frontal assignments.

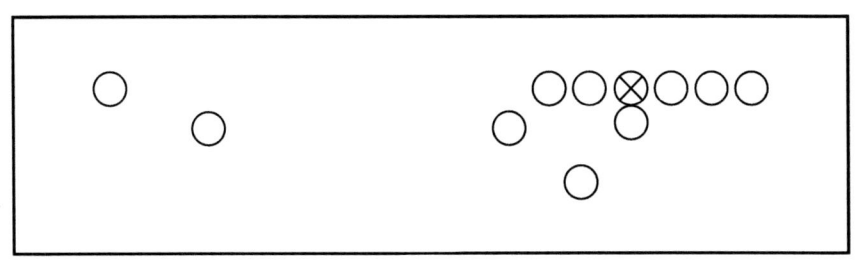

Diagram 4-5

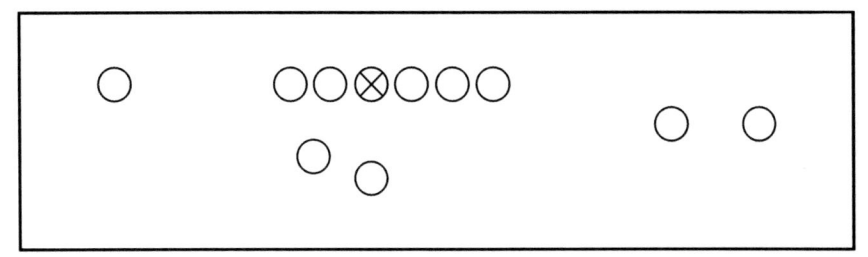

Diagram 4-6

7. The tight end can do three things:

   a. He can usually get to an end-of-line defender who might otherwise penetrate and keep the RB from getting all the way to the sideline on a wide run to stop the clock.

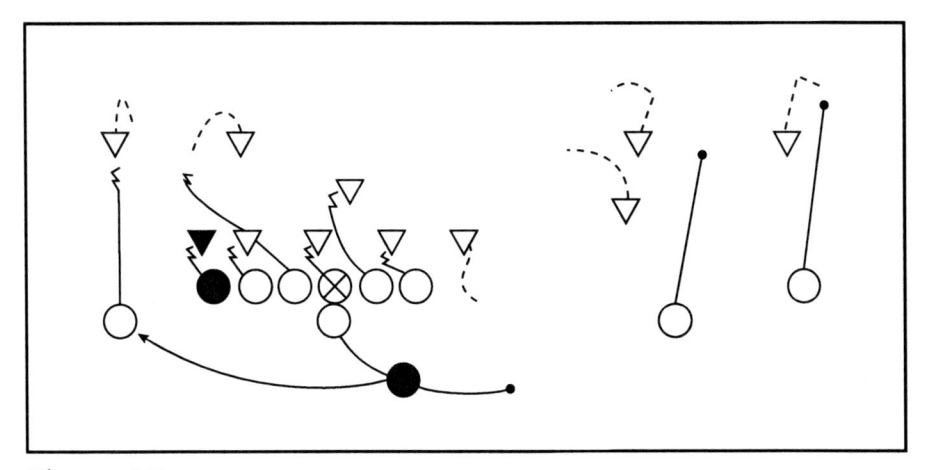

Diagram 4-7

b. In pass pro, when a blitz threatens, he can block a rusher while keeping a pass defender at bay with a delayed-pass threat. By occupying two defenders, he can eliminate the blitz threat. (The countering defensive tactic, seldom seen in a clock drive, is to play two pass defenders over him and rush with the one that he does not block.).

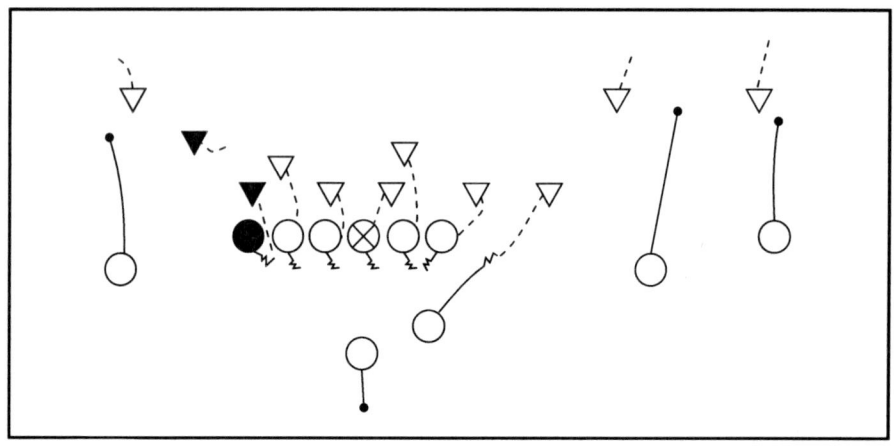

Diagram 4-8

c. On certain plays, when there is a true safety and when the defender over him must watch him in case of a flat pass, the TE can split out. This is effective on passes, the QB Draw, and certain plays that go the other way.

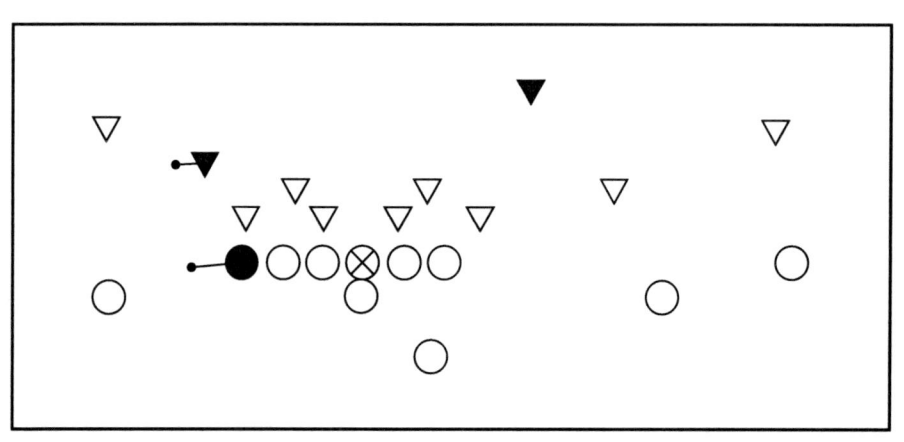

Diagram 4-9

Plays for clock offense should be selected from what the players know best.

Case: Air Force needs three points to tie Notre Dame. With 00:41, one time-out, and a first down on the Notre Dame 17, they run. The clock runs. They do not use the time-out. At 00:09 they run again, call time-out, kick, and tie. After the clock is turned off, in overtime, Notre Dame wins. Could Air Force have executed three runs and maybe gotten a touchdown? Yes, if just one of the first two gets the ball out-of-bounds. Boundary runs try to get the ball out-of-bounds, and they come into play when you do not want to pass and you are protected by a time-out. Here, one boundary run might have made the difference.

8. The offset running back's alignment pulls defenders toward him and, by doing so, makes it easier for blockers on the playside of his wide run to reach toward and engage defenders. The excellent bootleg threat that the offset position makes possible adds to the pull.

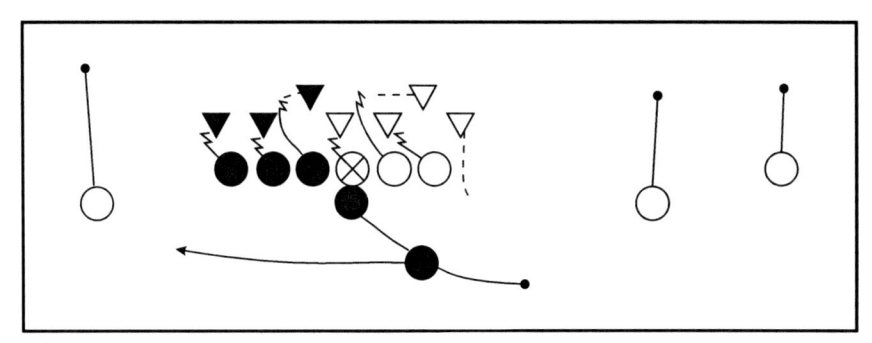

Diagram 4-10

9. The outside handoff-run must be combined with (a) the naked bootleg, shown in Figure 4-10, to keep the backside LB from mirroring the movement of the RB, and (b) a counter OT play on the side of the RB, shown in Figure 4-11, to discourage the positioning of an A-gap defender on the backside of the handoff run.

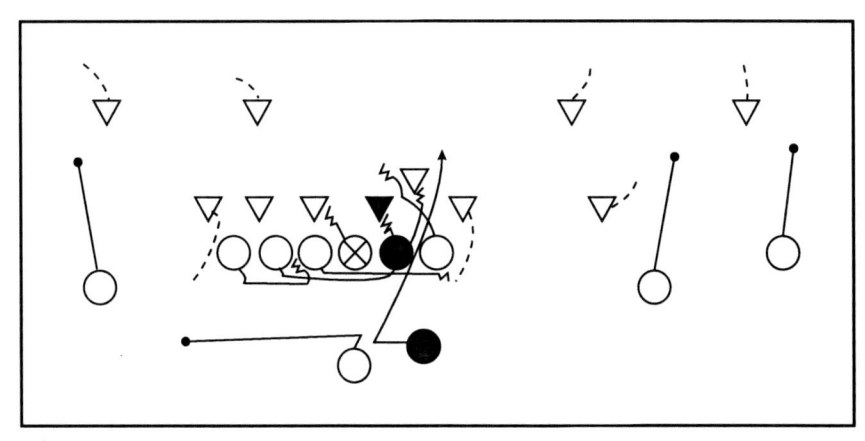

Diagram 4-11

10. The positions of the QB and RB, shown in Figure 4-12, make possible one of the best backfield fakes ever. A naked boot is the QB's threat and, out of the shotgun, he is in ideal position to confront pressure off the edge.

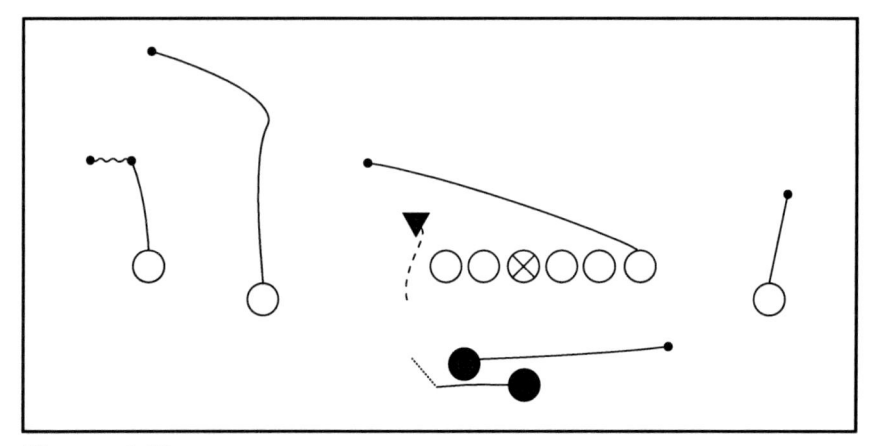

Diagram 4-12

11. Pass pro and a QB draw, shown in Figure 4-13, can look, initially, exactly alike.

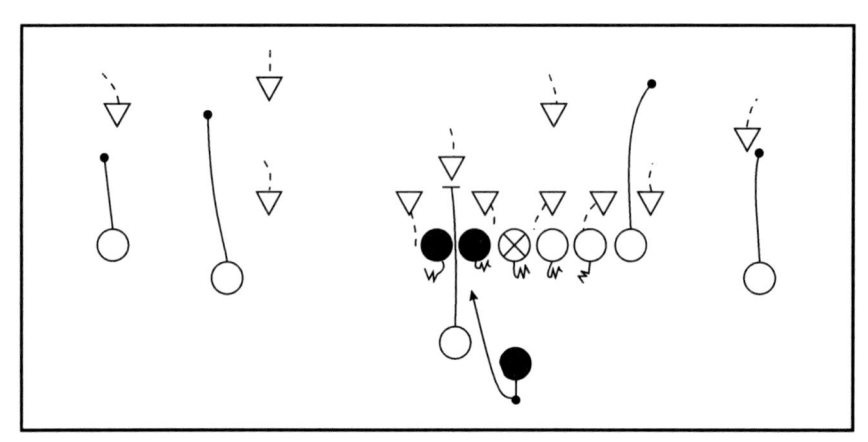

Diagram 4-13

12. A counter OT gets frontal defenders hit hard from the sides, shown in Figure 4-14. This affects the pass rush. When the QB is the ballcarrier, the unoccupied defender can be left far away from the point of attack.

13. The QB can, on most plays, go from either a shotgun or a tee position without changing a single assignment.

14. A sprintout run-or-pass option, shown in Figure 4-15, is a natural.

15. As a pass counter, the QB can sprint, stop on his 9th step, and lead the TE on a corner route, shown in Figure 4-16.

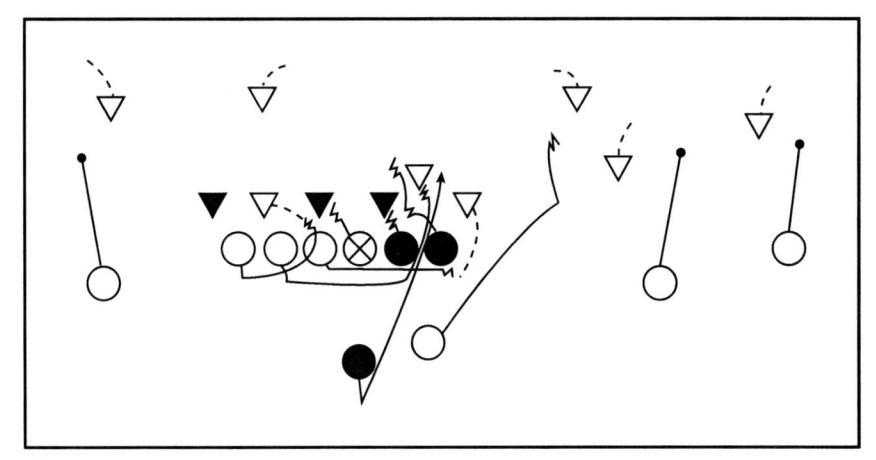

Diagram 4-14

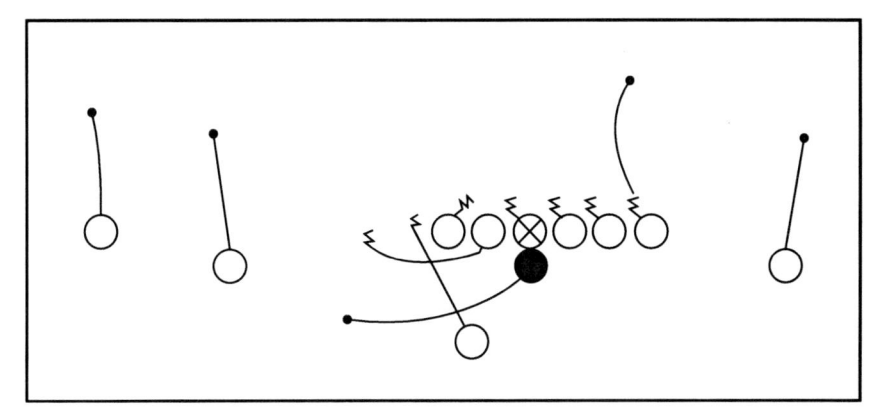

Diagram 4-15

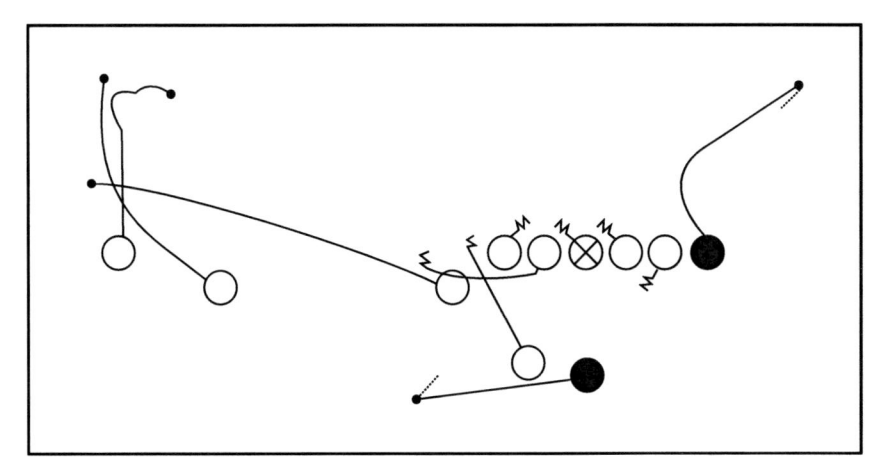

Diagram 4-16

16. As a run counter, the QB can hand back to the inside slotted back on a naked reverse, shown in Figure 4-17. It is a good 3rd-down play when the 4th-down play will be a FG from close in or a punt from your opponent's territory.

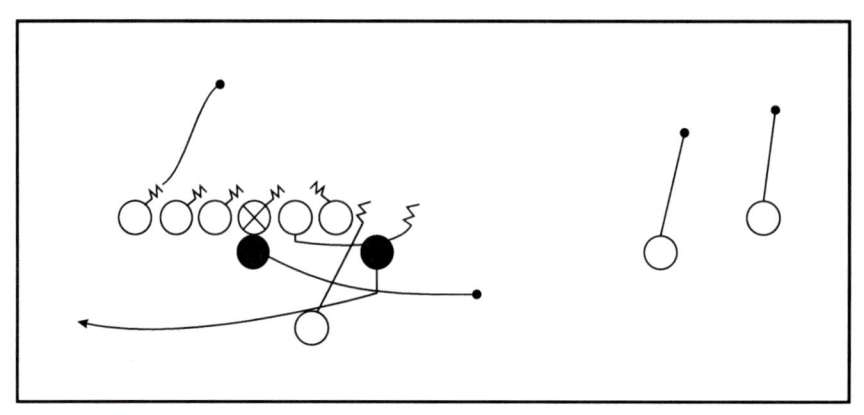

Diagram 4-17

Pointing, to Derive Assignments

Each play has one pivotal player. That player can initiate the targeting by pointing, just as one punt protector can.

1. Pivotal players for the plays suggested are,

    - to the slotted side, the called side,

        the sprintout run-or-pass—open-side tackle,

        the bootleg run-or-pass—center,

        the QB draw—center,

        the counter off-tackle run—open-side tackle,

        dropback protection—center, and

    - to the tight-end side, away from the called side,

        the inside hand-off run—center,

        the outside hand-off run—center,

        the option, out of the tee—tight end,

        the QB sneak, out of the tee—center, and

        the middle trap—center.

Pointing tells who one man will block, but it does not tell the defense (a) how or (b) whether the play is a run or a pass or (c) where the play is going.

After the center points to his dropback-pass target, the QB must point to any defender who can rush unblocked. This is for the benefit of any wide receiver who must get open if the unassigned man comes.

Examples of pivotal players and their targets, for a QB draw, shown in Figure 4-18, and an option play, shown in Figure 4-19, are isolated by darkened figures. Targetings for other plays are diagrammed in Appendix B.

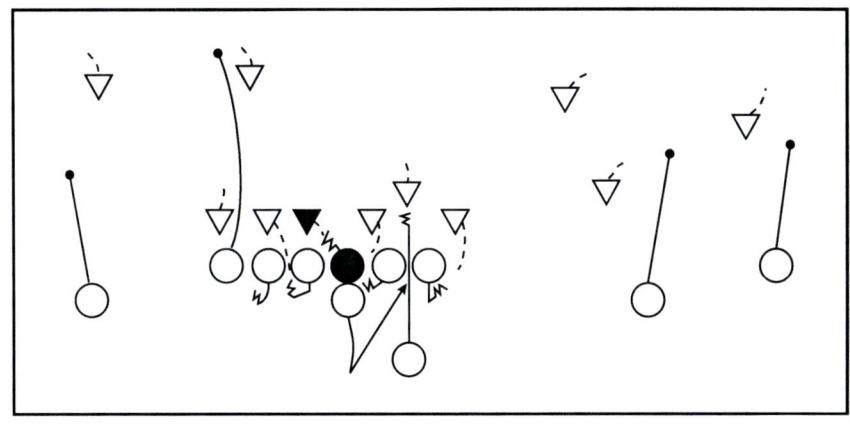

Diagram 4-18

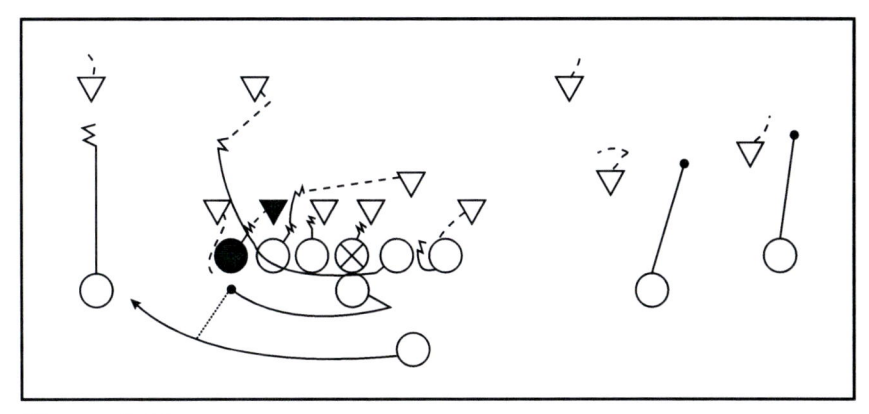

Diagram 4-19

Organizing a Dropback Protection

Having one frontal relationship, with the RB on one side and the TE on the other, requires that dropback pass protection and patterns be called to one side of that relationship. Calling them to the deployed end's side is best, in this basic clock formation, because it is usually the three-receiver side.

The two formations, shown in Figure 4-20 and Figure 4-21, have deployed backs together on both sides. One formation could be Left Trips, the other Left Flip. The protections for both, then, would be left. One pattern could be Teresa, for Trips; the other, Florence, for Flip. The relationship of receivers is the same in both pattern calls. (The relationship is not suitable for the first-down, boundary, or end-zone passes).

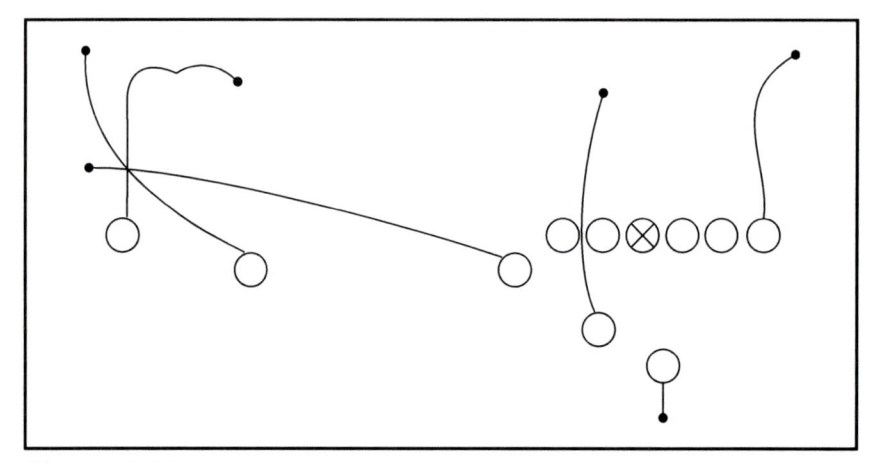

Diagram 4-20

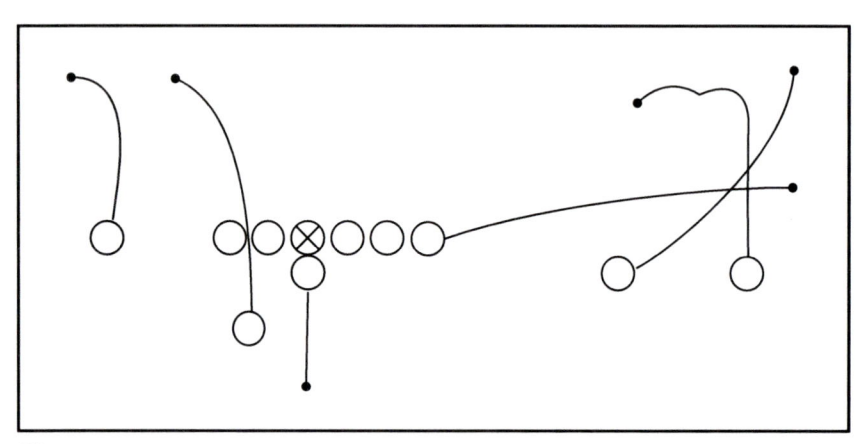

Diagram 4-21

Organizing Pass Patterns

Stop-the-clock offense is primarily passing offense. Failed passes stop the clock; failed runs do not. In a given amount of time and playing FAST, you can execute about twice as many passes as you can runs.

When the clock pressurizes passing, you want the passer and the five receivers to be doing familiar things. You do not want unfamiliar receiver relationships and passer timings. You especially want familiarity in special situations, such as

- when all five receivers must be able to catch and get out-of-bounds,
- when all five receivers must be at first-down depth,
- when space gets compressed and receivers must spread out in releasing, and
- when all five receivers must be at touchdown depth.

You want familiarity but results.

Case: Super Bowl, 2002. Tennessee Titans vs. St. Louis Rams. Titans, close to the Rams' goal line, need a TD. They have 00:06 on a stopped clock. The ball must go into the end zone with one of those several passes that take five seconds, or four. But the ball does not. The pass is completed short of the goal line, and the receiver goes down on the 6-inch line. The Titans lose.

Specifying First-Down and End-Zone Passes

The pattern shown in Figure 4-22 was shown as a feature of the formation. It occupies corners and puts three receivers beyond where LBers can cover. It can put the short receivers at first-down depth or at the goal-line flags.

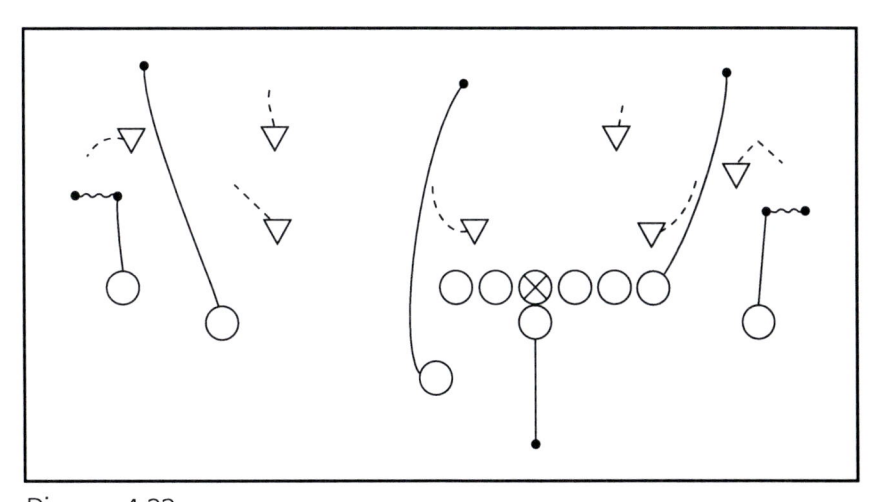

Diagram 4-22

A wide receiver hitches and slides to catch with his back to the cornerback, giving the ball the maximum stretch effect to the outside. A slotback or TE goes and gets a ball that is rifled to the sideline about 30 yards deep. He looks to the inside and catches with his back to the hitching receiver, again, giving the ball maximum stretch effect. The middle receiver races down the middle to catch a ball thrown to the exact middle of the field.

Case: Purdue is losing to Penn State in the fourth quarter, with 01:22 and no time-outs. The ball is on their two. They must go 70 yards to win with a FG. Penn State is all over the outside passes. The booth explains that those are the only passes available. That is wrong. Purdue throws incomplete passes and out-of-bounds and first-down passes for a mix of four, five, and six seconds of consumption. They execute 11 plays, with brilliant clock offense, but fail.

> **When you want all five receivers at first-down or touchdown depth, the problem is to keep them separated.**

The pattern shown in Figure 4-23 features crossing routes. It can adjust to first-down and end-zone depths.

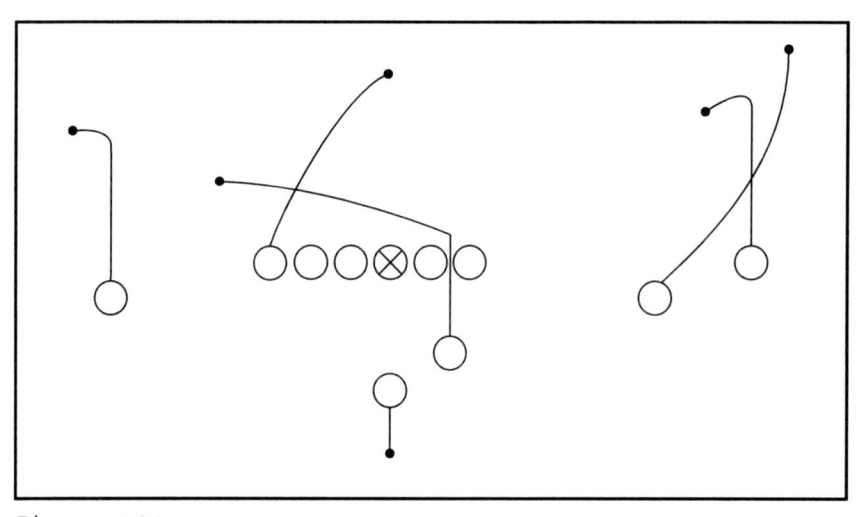

Diagram 4-23

The pattern shown in Figure 4-24 features option routes, with WRs fading. It, too, can adjust. The option routes can go to the first-down depth or beyond the goal line.

The idea of specifying first-down and end-zone passes is to give the passer no chance to throw a pass that will not stop the clock. The problem is keeping five receivers separated. Releasing only four receivers is not realistic.

Case: Marshall beats Toledo—49-45. Great offenses. Poor pass-pattern designs. Marshall, behind at 01:41, completes a pass for less than a first down and takes 42 seconds to get off the next play. Toledo, now behind at 00:46, throws for less

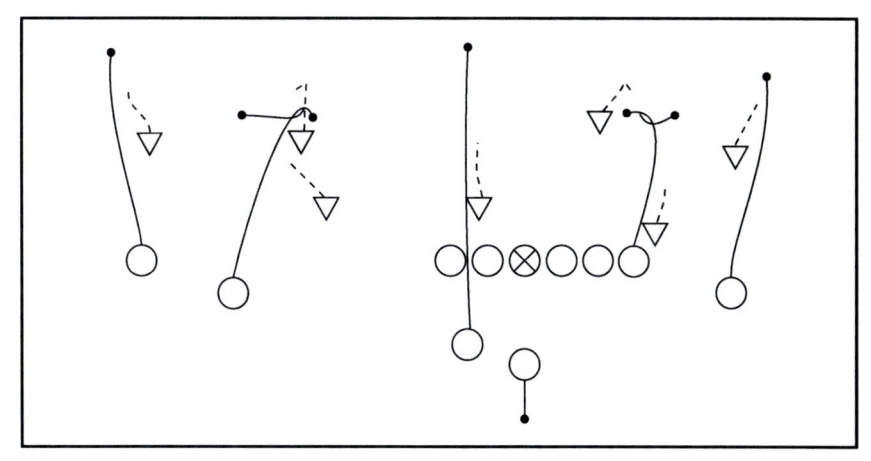

Diagram 4-24

than a first down and must use their last time-out. Toledo, with 00:30 and a first down, throws for less than a first down and spikes away their 2nd-down play.

The patterns with pairs of receivers on sidelines can be used for first downs only when the distance-to-go is 10 yards or less. The patterns that feature deep and dig routes should not be expected to adjust. Again, relationships and timings should always be familiar.

Specifying No Chance of Sack/Interception/Holding

The pattern shown in Figure 4-25 has two safe receivers and only two, plus a throw-away point. It leaves no chance of the QB throwing into a coverage he is not sure of and no chance that the ball will be held too long. The receivers can adjust. In an end zone the out route can come back to the goal-line flag.

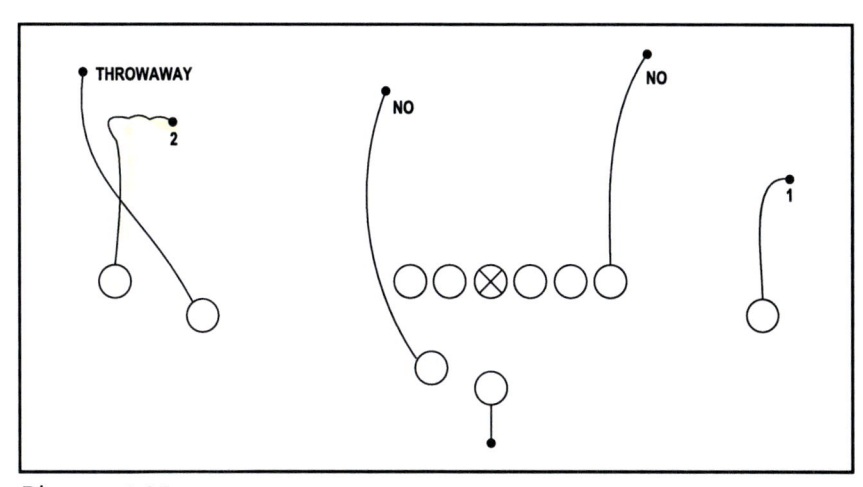

Diagram 4-25

> **When the clock pressurizes passing, you want the passer and all five receivers doing familiar things.**

Case: Auburn is playing Wyoming and trying to get at least a FG before halftime. They get a first down on the +28, with 00:17 and one time-out. They can call a pass that is designed to be either complete for a first down or incomplete but one with no chance of a sack, a holding penalty or an interception. Then, protected by the time-out, they can execute any play. What they do is squander seconds before a play, call the time-out after the play, kick from too far away, and miss.

Specifying Boundary Passes

The idea of having boundary passes is to give the passer only boundary receivers to throw to in situations where a pass must be either complete and out-of-bounds or incomplete.

Case: Behind Nebraska 24-31, Colorado takes over on their 32 with 05:20 and two time-outs. They want to score but not leave Nebraska time to score. At 00:53 they have 2nd-and-10 on the Nebraska 15. They have not saved too much time, because they may get a 1st-and-goal and need four plays. But they score, go for two, and go ahead by 32-31. The booth explains how much the victory will mean to Colorado and how, when Nebraska is in the shotgun, you have them right where you want them. On the Colorado 31, with a 1st-and-10 and 00:22, Nebraska runs its QB. The booth: "The play will be questioned." Nebraska calls its last time-out when the next Heisman Trophy winner fails to get a first down. Then they hit a boundary pass, kick at 00:05, and win 34-32.

> **In stop-the-clock offense, it is a lot easier to hit first-down passes than it is boundary passes.**

No new receiver relationships are needed. Only the idea of the passer looking only to sidelines is different. The receiver relationships shown are, to most passers, familiar. Sometimes, as shown in Figure 4-26, it helps get sideline receivers open by sending one receiver sprinting down the middle.

Sometimes, it helps to have two sideline receivers, two inside receivers to control the safeties, and the fifth receiver blocking. This was shown in Figure 4-2. There is only one way to put three receivers on a sideline. Figure 4-27 shows the way, with a fourth receiver controlling inside pass defenders.

There are two ways to put two receivers on a sideline. The patterns that put two or three receivers on sidelines should not be expected to adjust for first downs and touchdowns.

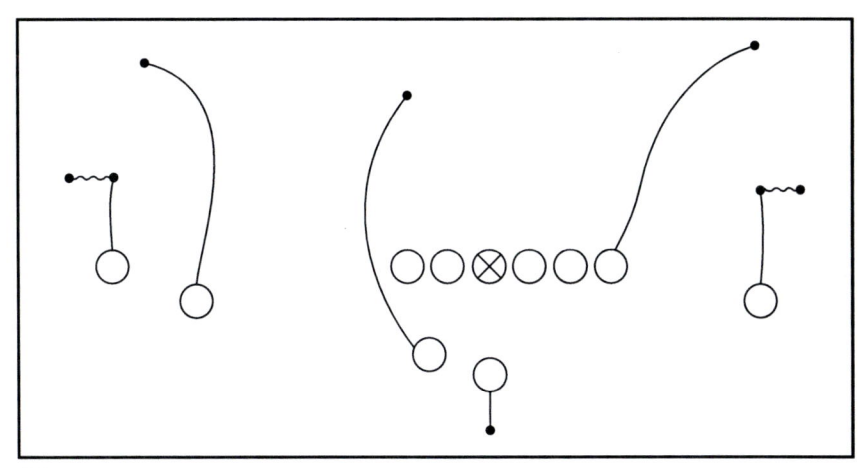

Diagram 4-26

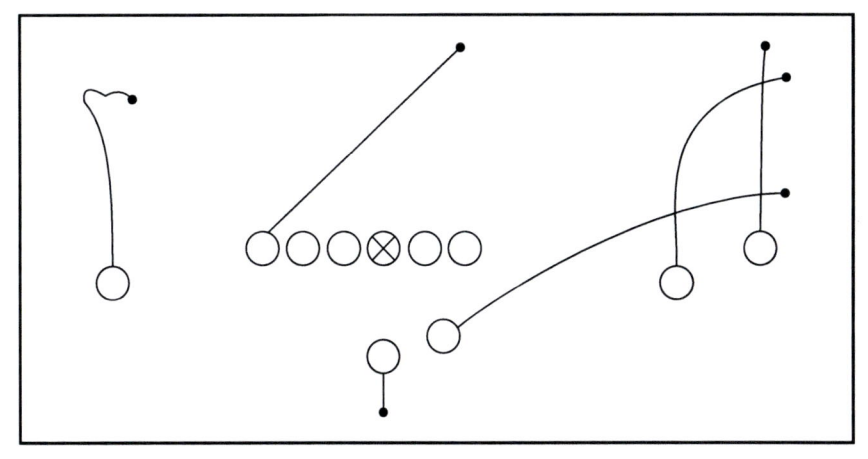

Diagram 4-27

Executing a Hail Mary

A Hail Mary pass needs about three seconds of protection. A shotgun QB can drop three steps, pop forward twice, throw high, and find a receiver 60 yards down the field. One receiver should have the ball dropped onto him, and three others should be positioned for the probable deflection. See Figure 4-28.

> **Case:** In the fourth quarter Kentucky has a first down on LSU's 30, tied, with 00:51. They throw, throw, run, run, get a first down on the 12, call their last time-out at 00:15, kick, and go ahead. The booth praises them for kicking on first down, in case

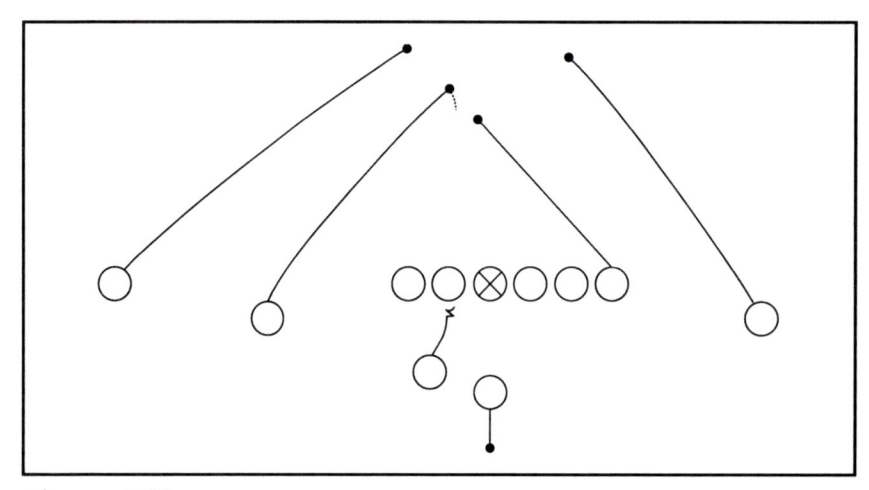

Diagram 4-28

there is a fumbled snap. But UK is out of time-outs. So is LSU. If there is a fumbled snap, there will not be another snap. Anyway, the UK players drench their coach with Gatorade. The booth jokes about needing more Gatorade to finish the job, calls the win miraculous, and reviews the game action. But UK has saved LSU some time instead of letting the clock go down to 00:04 before calling that time-out. UK kicks off. LSU returns to the 13. 00:09. Delay penalty. 17-yard pass. 00:02. Time-out. Hail Mary. Touchdown. Victory, LSU.

> ***Boundary, first-down, and end-zone passes are used to have zero chance of leaving the clock moving.***

Hand-Signaling

The one-handed, high-over-the-head signals for these stop-the-clock patterns should be distinctive and say that

- we are in stop-the-clock offense,
- the center, as the pivotal blocker, will point to his target,
- the QB will point to a possible blitzer, and
- the pattern signaled will be executed.

One straight arm over the head, using the thumb and the fingers, can call dropback protection and 10 patterns. One bent arm, with hand positions and touchings, can call the rest of the clock-offense plays.

5

Using the Intentional Incomplete Pass, the Spike

Assessing What a Spike Can Do

What can a spike do? Two things:

1. After the 15 seconds that you allow for the officials to get the ball ready, a spike starts you over and allows 35 more seconds for initiating the next play. It puts 50 seconds of real time between two of your plays. Without a spike, if you want to avoid wasting seconds, you have only 15 seconds of real time. It relieves pressure.

2. When you are out of time-outs, a spike can stop the clock to get field-goal personnel onto the field for an unhurried kick. When first-down yardage is needed for the kick, a spike is usually packaged with a pass that can get the first down. When less yardage or only better ball-position is needed, it is usually packaged with a 1st-down or 2nd-down run.

A spike puts 50 seconds of real time between two of your plays. It relieves pressure.

Measuring What a Spike Costs

When it is used to relieve pressure, it costs a lot. Why? Two reasons:

1. It costs one of the four downs that a first down earns you, and you almost never know that you will not need all four.

2. Even when there is not time to use all four downs and even if you can snap the ball for a regular play as fast as you can snap it for a spike, the throwing of the ball into the ground consumes a second or two that might have otherwise given you an additional play.

The only time you can spike without cost is when a first down leaves 00:05, 00:04, or 00:03 on a temporarily-stopped clock. These times allow only one more play, and you can spike and still have that play. With 00:06 you might get off a quick incomplete pass and have a second play; with 00:02, you might get off only the spike.

Case: San Diego State is behind Arizona State in the second quarter and gets a first down, with 00:18. They spike and go to 00:15 and, for all they know, to three plays instead of four. This is not fair to the players.

Case: Washington vs. Michigan. Michigan passes for a first down on the five, going in, and has 30 seconds left. The booth: "Michigan doesn't have to be in that big of a hurry." Michigan hurries but spikes and, in doing so, gives up 25 per cent of their possible plays.

Following are comparisons that show how a spike can cost a play. The following series both begin with temporarily-stopped clocks, at 00:19. The assumptions in the numbers are that a snap after a temporary stop will take one second, that an incomplete pass will take six, and that a spike will take only one.

00:19, clock temporarily stopped

you snap at 00:18	you snap at 00:18
you pass, incomplete 00:12 remains	you spike 00:17 remains
you pass, incomplete 00:06 remains	you pass, incomplete 00:11 remains
you pass, incomplete 00:00 remains	you pass, incomplete 00:05 remains
	you pass, incomplete 00:00 remains

In this first comparison, three passes are thrown in each series. The spike does **not** cost a play.

The following series both begin with temporarily-stopped clocks, at 00:20.

00:20, clock temporarily stopped

you snap at 00:19	you snap at 00:19
you pass, incomplete 00:13 remains	you spike 00:18 remains
you pass, incomplete 00:07 remains	you pass, incomplete 00:12 remains
you pass, incomplete 00:01 remains	you pass, incomplete 00:06 remains
you pass, touchdown	you pass, incomplete 00:00 remains

In this second comparison, in the no-spike series (left) the fourth pass scores; in the spike series (right) a fourth pass is never thrown. The spike does cost a play.

> ***Even if you cannot use all four downs, a spike consumes a second or two that might have otherwise allowed you an additional play.***

Adding Seconds with a Spike

Can seconds be added with a spike? Yes. If initiating a play after the ball is declared ready takes more time than finishing a spike, time will be saved by the spike, although the fourth play in the series will be lost. If initiating a play takes six additional seconds and if the fourth play is not needed for a first down, a hurried spike will add four or five seconds. The following comparison is between a series that begins with a delayed snap (left) and a series that begins with a quick spike (right).

00:18, clock stopped temporarily

you snap, delayed, at 00:12	you snap at 00:17
you pass, incomplete 00:06 remains	you spike 00:16 remains
you pass, incomplete 00:00 remains	you pass, incomplete 00:10 remains
	you pass, incomplete 00:04 remains
	you pass, touchdown

In the delayed-snap series, a third pass is never thrown; in the spike series, the third pass scores.

Getting the Ball-Ready Signal

The ref starts the 25-second counter by dropping his hand and tooting his whistle. The hand is for the clock operator; the toot is for the players. The Ref is not responsible for being in the center's or the QB's field of vision when he drops his hand; and the toot can, sometimes, be drowned out by crowd noise. A solution for spiking, in extreme noise, is for the QB to be under the center, to have his team ready, to twist around and watch the Ref, and to call for the snap as the hand drops.

Considering What to Do

Should a spike be able to do more than put the ball into the ground? What if you are spiking to relieve pressure and a deployed receiver is uncovered? Should the QB be able to throw to him? No. Why? Two reasons:

- One kind of spike will do—the kind that will predictably consume two seconds.
- Also, the easiest protection for a spike is cup protection, like for extra points and field goals, and this protection will leave end-of-line defenders unblocked and make throwing to a deployed receiver difficult.

> ***A spike should be used for getting field-goal personnel onto the field and for little else.***

Keeping Time from Expiring on a Spike

The QB does not want to take a snap for a spike unless the snap will have at least 00:03. If it would have only 00:02, he wants the ball to go to the end zone.

The solution is to have an end-zone-pass/spike package and, when you are concerned, to call for the package and have the QB prepare to throw for the end zone but to go to the spike on his own if he has 00:03 or more.

Case: In a span of five years, two Rose Bowl games end with spike calls, without the ball getting to the end zone even though there is time to throw it there. One ends after a first-down clock shows 00:02.

Bleeding the Clock, then Spiking

To use a time-out, the QB should bleed down to 00:04. To call for the snap for a field goal, the holder should do the same. To call for the snap on a spike play, however, the QB should bleed down only to 00:06.

Comparing Hurrying-On with Spiking, to Get FG Personnel On

A hurry-on takes 20 seconds from the time a play ends. A spike takes almost that long, with 15 seconds of it being the ref's time. A hurry-on usually comes after a 3rd-down play. A spike always comes after a 1st-down or a 2nd-down play.

Ensuring Against Spiking on a 4th Down

How do you keep a QB from spiking on 4th down and, unintentionally, turning the ball over? You do not let him decide on using it. You think of it as being paired the way a next-to-last play and a final play are paired. You think of a pair as a 1st- or 2nd-down pair only. You think of the 3rd down as different. You learn to anticipate a spike one play ahead of time and to call it in a pair. You teach other players to recognize a mistake. You test to ensure that an approach to a mistake will be arrested. You explain that football history has enough 4th-down spikes.

Good QBs want plays, not spikes. Just ask one.

Learning from Cases

Spiking is for getting field-goal personnel onto the field. Using it for anything else can be costly.

> **Case:** Georgia, against Auburn, throws for the end zone four times and hits on the fourth for a touchdown, getting a victory with the down that so many teams use up with a spike.

> Case: In an Independence Bowl, Iowa State needs a field goal to beat Alabama. They get a first down, short of the field-goal line. Their time-outs are gone, but there is time for three plays and a kick. They spike when the clock is stopped for the first

down—they spike away one-third of the offense they have for getting closer. After two plays they kick on 4th down from too far away, miss, and lose.

Case: Ohio State is going to win. Michigan is going to run out of time. With 00:20 on their 46, Michigan spikes away a down and one second. Later, with a first down and 00:09 on the OSU 24, they spike away two seconds. After an incomplete pass at 00:01, they have a final 3rd-down chance, but they fail. Here, the wasted three seconds did not make a difference to Michigan, but they might have.

Coaches call for spiking to relieve pressure.

Case: Louisville 25, East Carolina 28, fourth quarter, 01:23. Louisville is on the ECU 31, with one time-out and a first down. They run for a yard. The QB is back on the line. On the sideline, one coach is pointing to his watch; another is making the spiking motion. The QB spikes. Trying to get a little closer to kick and tie, the QB is made to throw one-half of his chances into the turf. On 3rd-down, a sack. On 4th, a Hail Mary, out-of-bounds.

Case: Michigan hits a long second-quarter pass on the Florida eight, with 00:34 and one time-out. There is a signal from the sideline to spike. The QB does. The 4th down will be used for a FG, so the QB has thrown one-third of his chances into the ground. There is no redeeming factor in doing this. It is inconsiderate and wrong.

So do TV commentators.

Case: Maryland, against Georgia Tech, has 2nd-and-10 on the +28, with 22 seconds left. The booth: "They should spike on 3rd down and decide what to do."

Case: In the 2nd quarter the Green Bay Packers have the ball on the Carolina Panthers' 45, with 00:25. Brett Favre throws deep. The booth says he should have spiked. Favre, with time to throw four passes, should throw one of them into the ground?

Most spiking is mismanaging, not managing, the clock.

6

Using Time-Outs

Case: In the 2000 Super Bowl, time expires with the Tennessee Titans on the St. Louis Rams' six-inch line. The Titans had another down. Could they have had a few more seconds? They start the drive with one time-out. One had been wasted in the third quarter. Anyway, they use that last time-out on a play that does not stop the clock, and they spike once. The time-out that was wasted earlier would have given them another play and, probably, the victory.

Reviewing Situational Uses

All kinds of situations call for time-outs. In a partial list, here are 11:

- You need a touchdown to win and have a 1st-and-goal on the two, with 00:19 on a first-down clock. With three time-outs you can run four times. With no time-outs you can pass four times but run only once.

- You are behind by eight in the fourth quarter and have a 4th-and-10 on your opponent's 12, with 02:31 on a stopped clock. Can you kick, make it minus five, kick off, stop him, stop the clock, take his punt, drive, and win? It depends on your time-outs. If you do not have at least two, you need to gamble, now, on making the toughest 12 yards in football, making a two-pointer, and having a 50 percent chance of winning in overtime.

> ***A time-out can stop the clock at any time except during the execution of a play.***

- You have a strong wind behind you near a change of quarters, with 3rd-and-one and 00:16 on a stopped clock. You do not want to pass, even though it would keep you from having to punt against the wind. But, if you run, failure would let the quarter end and put the wind against you. An available time-out would allow you to run, fail, stop the clock anyway, and punt with the wind.

- You are behind and your opponent is in SLOW play, executing a play every 45 seconds. One time-out could save you 40 seconds and add six or seven clock-stopping plays to the drive that you must have. If you get the ball and go into FAST play and are executing a play every 20 seconds, that same time-out would save you only 15 seconds and add only two or three clock-stopping plays.

- You are behind by a touchdown and driving. You want to have time to execute four runs if you get a 1st-and-goal. If you have three time-outs, you need to save only 20 seconds. If you have no time-outs, you need to save 70 seconds. If you need to save only 20, to score on the 1st-and-goal play would be to leave the opponent 15 seconds to answer. If you need to save 70, to score on that play would be to leave him 65.

- You are within FG range, with a 2nd-down and 00:46, 00:45. You need a FG to win. If you have a time-out, you can safely run twice either to get closer and position the ball or to use up excess time. A time-out can stop the clock at any time except during the execution of a play.

- You have a 4th-and-13 on your 32, with 02:29 on a stopped clock. It is in the fourth quarter, and you are down by two. If you have three time-outs, you can punt, limit your opponent's time consumption to about 40 seconds, and leave yourself time to take his punt, drive, and get a FG.

- You are behind by one. There is 01:29 left on a stopped clock. The opponent has the ball, 1st down, on his 29. If you have no time-outs, he can take a knee and win. If you have three, he must get a first down to keep you from getting the ball and having more than a minute for your drive.

- Your opponent is within chip-shot range of a winning FG, and he threatens to bleed away the seconds you would need for answering with your own FG. Only time-outs can staunch the bleeding.

- It is 4th down, fourth quarter, with 00:38, 00:37 as the 3rd-down play ends. You are within FG range and need three points to win. Your opponent has no time-outs. If you have a time-out, you can securely bleed through the ref's time and on through most of the 25-second counter, call the time-out at 00:04, kick for three, and leave him with 00:00.

> **When you are behind, one time-out called on your opponent's SLOW play can save you 40 seconds and add six or seven clock-stopping plays to your necessary drive.**

For managing the clock, you need time-outs. They are precious.

Case: It is Michigan 7, Wisconsin 7 in the fourth quarter. Michigan gets the ball on their 20, with 01:26. What should Wisconsin do? They want Michigan to run out of time before they can kick a FG; but if a FG is good, they want to have time to answer. So, they should hold onto their time-outs and hope Michigan stalls. If Michigan gets to FG range, they should use their time-outs. This is to gamble that they can keep Michigan from getting closer, consuming time, and making answering more difficult. Meanwhile, Michigan is forced to punt, with 01:05, 01:04. Should Wisconsin call time-out on the punt? Yes. But they do not. Why? Tension. The bouncing punt is touched by a Wisconsin player, within FG range. Michigan falls on the ball, kicks, and wins.

Case: Cincinnati, ahead of Ohio State 12-7 in the second quarter, has a first down on the 50, with 00:26 and one time-out. QB scramble. Down at 00:20. Time-out at 00:12. Seven seconds wasted. Pass incomplete. Pass incomplete again. Fourth down at 00:01. How close were they to losing that 4th down by not calling the time-out as soon as the QB went down?

Using the First Two Time-Outs

If you have a question about when to use time-outs, ask a good QB. He will tell you to use them to give him more time to execute plays, not to give you more time to decide on plays.

Might using time-outs save time for your opponent to answer your score with his score? Yes. Do you consider this? Only after using them to save yourself enough time to execute every play that your first downs will allow.

Would you ever use time-outs on him in the second quarter? Before a 4th-down punt, maybe. Remember, however, that you do not have to score in the second quarter to win. If you use one on him after a 1st-, 2nd-, or 3rd-down play, there is a chance that he will make a good gain on his next play and have the saved time to add plays to his own drive. It is different in the fourth quarter when you are behind and must score to win.

Is it wasteful to "take time-outs to your locker room?" Not necessarily. Not if you might have needed them.

Is it risky to use a second-half time-out before the end of the fourth quarter? Yes. It may have been the time-out that you will needed to add plays on a final drive.

> **A good QB will want you to use time-outs to give him more plays, not to give you more time to think and confer.**

Accept that you cannot always save three time-outs for clock offense. You would use one

- to get a punt off with the wind before a change of quarters, or
- to save your offense or defense from a substitution mistake.

Using the Third Time-Out

Having one time-out at the end of a stop-the-clock drive makes all plays the same in the time it takes to use them as next-to-the-last plays. Having one takes a lot of the difficulty out of finishing a drive.

To stop the clock without a time-out, you have only the spike, which (a) has to wait for the ball to be declared ready, (b) takes one or two seconds, and (c) cannot follow a 3rd-down play.

When you are behind, do you use the third time-out the way you use the other two, to add plays? Yes. Called on your opponent, it can add six or seven clock-stopping plays to your drive. You almost always use it.

You do not always use it on your own FAST offense. If you expect your next-to-the-last play to be a run to position the ball for a FG kick, you can save it to get the FG personnel onto the field. There, the time-out will keep you from needing 20 seconds to hurry on the personnel and, used earlier, it would have saved only 20 seconds. So, you use it and, later, hurry on; or you save it and, later, you do not have to hurry on.

What can you lose by saving your last time-out for your field goal?

1. If you would have used it on your own FAST offense to save 15 seconds and if you do use it to stop the clock to get field-goal personnel on, you lose essentially nothing.

2. If you could have used it on your own FAST offense but did not, and then if you do not need it to stop the clock in the same series for a planned 4th-down kick, you lose nothing. You got to the 4th-down kick.

3. If you could have used it on your opponent's SLOW offense and saved 40 seconds and if you do use it on your FAST offense and save 15, you lose a net 25.

Suggestion: Use your last time-out to save 40 seconds, in any situation. Use it to save 15 seconds only if you expect to be passing for boundaries or first-down lines to get to field-goal position; otherwise, save it for the field goal. Just do not, by a simplistic rule, save it for the field goal.

Having a time-out enables you to use any play as a next-to-the-last play. As long as you get the ball snapped with 00:10 on the clock and the ballcarrier does not zig and zag, you can call the time-out and, then, call whatever play you want.

Case: A great Florida State team needs a touchdown to beat Miami and gets a 1st-and-goal on the 10, with a time-out and 00:10. They can start a play at 00:09, execute it, call the time-out, and get a second play. As it is, they let the clock go down to 00:05, call the time-out, fail with their only play, and suffer their only loss of the season.

For additional cases see Appendix C.

Being Out Of Time-Outs

Correlated with using that last time-out is having already used it and, then, not having it. When it is gone, barriers appear beyond which you cannot go with a next-to-the-last play that would leave a temporarily-stopped or a moving clock. They are:

- from a stopped to a first-down—00:15,
- from a stopped to a moving—00:25,
- from a first-down to a first-down—00:20,
- from a first-down to a moving—00:30,
- from a moving to a first-down—00:30,
- from a moving to a moving—00:40.

A conservative assumption in these numbers is that it takes five seconds to get the ball snapped after it is declared ready following a first down. The play is estimated to take 10 seconds. The ref, 15.

> *Having a time-out takes a lot of the difficulty out of finishing a stop-the-clock drive.*

Using the Time-Out in Each Extra Period

In an extra period everything is different, because the clock is turned off. But is there a way to use a time-out to maximum advantage? Your choices are to use it to

- review a final play,
- review a two-point play,
- "ice" an opponent field-goal kicker, or
- ensure against executing in confusion.

It would not be wise to use it on your own field-goal and unwittingly "ice" your own kicker. If your opponent uses his on your field goal, your kicker wants to have a well-timed practice routine, so there will be no "icing" effect. Maximum advantage? You decide.

7

Distinguishing Between Procedures and Decisions

Approaching and Practicing Them Differently

In clock offense there are procedures, and there are decisions. The two must be approached differently, and they must be practiced differently.

Playing FAST is a procedure. Using a reference point to tell you which kind of play can be executed in the remaining time is procedural. Choosing to run and have one chance to score rather than to pass and have three chances is a decision. Taking a safety rather than punting, because of (a) the time remaining, (b) the point differential, and (c) your opponent's time-outs, is decisional.

Case: In 1999 Notre Dame loses to Purdue and is widely criticized for poor clock management. An examination of the game's play-by-play reveals that classic dilemma: the clock calls for passing while success on the immediate drive calls for running. ND makes a decision to run, as many would have, and "runs" out of time.

Procedures can be pressure-packed and can make your clock management look smart, but they are straightforward and can be agreed upon ahead of time. Decisions involve clock times and at least two other factors, and the possibilities for them are obscured in relationships among variables.

> *Procedures and decisions in clock management are different. They must be approached and practiced differently.*

Separating Them

Using a time-out against your opponent's offense is a procedure. It is smart clock management, but it involves no decision. Bleeding the clock is a procedure. Spiking should be a procedure. Choosing to punt rather than go for a first down, after considering (a) the distance to go, (b) the time, (c) the opponent's time-outs, and (d) the point differential, is a decision. Choosing to run for a touchdown, rather than pass and risk saving your opponent 30 extra seconds for his clock offense, is a decision.

Characteristic of procedures is that coaches generally agree on them. Characteristic of decisions is that there are decision points where five of 10 coaches would choose one way and five would choose the other. For you, these points are like watersheds, where you could go either way but where you must go one way or the other, right now.

Case: Ahead by three, with 4th-and-one on its 39 and 00:40 left in a game against Clemson, Georgia calls time-out. The booth: "They'd better punt." And, "I can't imagine going for it." Clemson is out of time-outs. There would be an eleven-man rush against a punt, and probably the only way for Clemson to win the game outright is to block a punt. Georgia's decision: Go. They do. And win.

Procedures will not involve two courses that look equally right. Decisions can. Decisions can require immediate deciding even when you are not sure which way is the right way but when the wrong way is any delayed way.

> *When a coach takes and wastes a time-out, it is often because he must make a decision and there is no obviously right one.*

Procedures can be practiced until you master them, until you know exactly what you will do in each situation. Decisions must be practiced in simulation, where you can be led to dilemmatic decision-points, over and over again, until you can quickly make decisions when there are no clearly right decisions.

All run-or-pass questions are decisional. As are these three questions: Kick a FG or go for it? Let him or do not let him score? Kick an extra point or take a knee?

Keeping the clock moving is procedural, until it becomes a run-or-pass question. Taking a safety is procedural in a few situations but decisional in most.

The point of separating them is simply that you do not want to confront watershed decisions without a lot of separate practice in avoiding indecision.

Case: Auburn gets the ball on the LSU 49 in the second quarter, with 01:34 and one time-out. Later, with a 2nd-and-10 on the 22, they hit a seven-yard pass and use the time-out at 00:44. Wise decision? It is 3rd-and-three. Compare: Do not take the time-out, and a run or pass for a first down leaves about 00:23—time for two end-zone or boundary passes, one run, a time-out, and a kick. Or, take the time-out, and a first down leaves about 00:38—time for two boundary or end-zone passes, one run, a hurry-on, and a kick. Wise? Some would say yes; some, no.

Procedures and decisions mostly, although not always, separate themselves. What separate practice does is encourage high-repetition work on decisions. What such work will do is let you experience, for example, a fourth-quarter 4th down that is four feet short of the agreed-upon FG line and two feet short of the first-down line, and, being behind by two points with 00:41, 00:40 and no time-outs. What it will do is let you experience deciding in two seconds (a) to kick from beyond the FG line or (b) to run for two feet and, if successful, spike and kick, or (c) to ensure that the ball will get to the end zone by going ahead and throwing an end-zone pass.

Locating Watersheds in Decision Possibilities

Here are three decision-making problems that would divide experienced coaches:

Situation: Near the end of the third quarter, you have 3rd-and-one on your 38, with 00:26, 00:25, the score tied, and a strong wind at your back.

Choices: (a) Pass and, if you fail, have the wind at your back for a punt, or (b) run with a better chance of making it and, if you fail, either burn a time-out or change ends of the field and have the wind in your face for your punt.

Situation: Fourth quarter. You have 4th-and-nine on your two, with 00:38 on a stopped clock. You are ahead by three. Your opponent has two time-outs.

Choices: (a) Punt and risk either a block for seven points and your defeat or your opponent kicking a field goal and sending you into an extra period, or (b) take a safety, keep a one-point lead, and fight to keep him from taking your free kick, coming back, and getting a field goal to win.

Situation: 1st-and-goal on his two-foot line, fourth quarter. You are down by six, with 00:18 on the temporarily-stopped clock and no time-outs.

Choices: (a) Pass and risk the sack/holding/interception possibilities but, if you fail, have another play, or (b) run and, if you fail, lose the game.

> *You cannot get comfortable with decision-making without repetitious table-top simulations of game action.*

Practicing

You cannot get enough decision-making practice without committing yourself to simulation. Here is an example of what you can do in simulation:

- You move down the field with no time-outs and the game ending, get past the FG line with 3rd down and 00:42, 00:41, call a run, execute it, see 00:22, 00:21, hurry FG personnel on, kick, win, and "push the reset button." This time you get to the 3rd down with 00:38, 00:37.

What you do in simulation is get yourself led into dilemmas and make decisions. If a dilemma ties you up and threatens to make you waste time or call time-out, you "push the reset button," which is to say that you have your assistant start you over. You do this until you are sure that indecision by you in a game will not cost your team precious seconds.

> *You have to be ready to make a quick decision when there is no obviously right decision.*

For more situations and decisions see Appendix D.

8

Clarifying Objectives

Listing Them

The general objective of stop-the-clock offense is

- to ensure a final try for the points needed, and
- to get all that the clock will allow before that try.

Specific objectives can be

- a touchdown,
- a field goal,
- a TD, but settle for a FG,
- a FG, but go first for a TD,
- to begin stop-the-clock offense but be ready to switch to move-the-clock,
- to begin move-the-clock offense but be ready to switch to stop-the-clock, and
- to punt with the wind.

Case: Georgia 10, Florida 12, second quarter. Georgia picks up a fumble and gets a 1st-and-goal on the five. They have 01:11 and one time-out. The objective is to try to get a TD but, for sure, to get a FG and have a halftime lead. They can try to play fast and get in three 20-second runs and a final play. If they fall behind the 20-second schedule, they can insert an end-zone pass. What actually happens is less-than-fast play, a penalty, less than prompt calling of the time-out, but a 4th-down kick and a halftime lead.

Urgency levels might be separated according to where you

- pass, run wide, hustle,
- do not huddle when the clock is moving,
- run or pass to boundaries, pass to first-down lines, use time-outs, and get ready to (a) squeeze in a next-to-the-last play or (b) use the spike to get field-goal personnel on or (c) hurry on field-goal personnel or (d) use an interruption snap before the ball is declared ready.

Speeds of play have been suggested, in seconds between snaps, as

FAST—20,

HUSTLE—25,

NORMAL—30 to 35

DELIBERATE—40, and

SLOW—45.

Clock offense can begin in the last five minutes of clock time, although the important procedures and decisions are concentrated in the last 30 seconds.

In college, as of 2008, there is a new rule for out-of-bounds balls. Late in the second and fourth quarters, if a stopped game clock reads (a) 2:00 or (b) 1:59, the (a) clock starts when the ball is ready for play, but the (b) clock starts on the snap. In other words, inside of two minutes, an out-of-bounds ball is going to stop the clock and keep it stopped until the snap.

> ***To refer to stop-the-clock offense as two-minute offense is misleading. To refer to move-the-clock offense as four-minute offense is just as misleading.***

Communicating Objectives

Two-handed signals for giving the QB the speeds of play might be, at waist height,

- hands making small and fast circles with elbows out for FAST,
- demonstrative clapping hands for HUSTLE,
- two open hands with thumbs out for NORMAL,
- hands moving up and down at stepping speed for DELIBERATE, and
- hands in slow, smoothing motions for SLOW.

Words to a QB on the sideline should be in three parts:

- the objective,
- what you want him to say as the leader, and
- what he may be called on to do in the final seconds.

First, the objective should be specific; not, "We're in two-minute offense." Examples:

- "We need to start thinking about the clock. I'll call more passes and wide runs. For you, though, the next drive is just normal."
- "We want a touchdown. We'll kick a field goal only if we're close enough and it's fourth-and-too-much. Close enough is the fifteen."
- "Let's start with fast play but be ready to switch if we have excess time."
- "We need a field goal. Once we get to the 20, no more passes or options."
- "Let's start taking more time. You keep it deliberate, until I signal otherwise."
- "Down by nine—three twenty left. We're in fast play—tell the guys. Save the time-outs for when they have the ball."
- "If we have to punt, we want it to be after the quarter so we will be with the wind. Just play football, but take the twenty-five-second counter down to four or three."
- "We don't need to play fast yet, but keep signaling to the guys that we're in a hustle mode."

> *At the end of a stop-the-clock drive, you want the ball to be in the end zone, by a play or a kick.*

Case: West Virginia trails Syracuse 10-17 in the second quarter and has the ball on their 11, with two time-outs and 02:16. They proceed to make first downs and consume the time that they do not want Syracuse to have. Near midfield they transition to stop-the-clock offense. They use a time-out on their 39, after a 1st-down play, and have 00:21. They run to their 43 and use their last time-out at 00:15. Tension mounts. Talk from the booth is about the food in the pressbox at halftime. With time-outs gone, UWV hits a 24-yard pass with 00:05 on a clock that will start on the ready. They hurry FG personnel on, kick for three, and go to the locker room pumped about going 89 yards in two minutes, getting on the scoreboard, and leaving Syracuse with no time to answer.

Second, instructions to the QB should be to say whatever you would say if you could be on the field. Examples:

- "Remind the skill guys to get out-of-bounds if they don't have a first down but to stay inbounds and fight for yardage if they do."
- "Remind the receivers on the first-down passes to get all of the underneath routes beyond the first-down line."
- "Remember, on a measurement or a penalty, get lined up, take my signal, and get the play called. I'll give you another play if the chains or the ball gets moved."
- "Tell everybody that this is the no-hold, no-sack, no-interception pass."
- "We're in fast play. Tell the guys to land in place. Use time-outs as soon as you need them. We are not saving a time-out."
- "Huddle on out-of-bounds or incomplete. I'll send in a play. If in doubt about out-of-bounds near the first-down line, don't huddle."
- "If you have different personnel and you don't get an out-of-bounds or an incomplete, I'll have clock personnel back on immediately. You just stay with fast play. The guys'll get off and on."
- "Stay on the line even after an out-of-bounds or an incomplete pass. We've got 'em rattled. Remind the guys—we want a picture of pace and poise."

Case: Pittsburgh, down by seven in the second quarter against Texas A&M, has the ball on its own 10, with 00:54 and three time-outs. They pass. Wise? Most coaches would say, no; not from the 10; do not give A&M the ball plus good field position.

Third, any reminder of what the QB may have to do should be vivid. Examples:

- "At the end, remember, if we miscalculate and you see fifteen or less on a moving clock, call for the interruption snap."

- "You can throw four passes into the end zone in 16 seconds. You just make sure you don't get sacked."
- "The barriers for a boundary pass are twenty-five and fifteen. I may fudge a little but, if you think you need to change to an end-zone pass, you do it." (Twenty-five, he knows, is the barrier for a clock-stopping pass out of a moving clock; fifteen, for a clock-stopping pass out of a first-down clock.)
- "We have three time-outs so we only need thirty seconds for four plays inside the ten. As long as we have thirty for each play outside the ten, I will give you the deliberate-play signal."
- "We won't throw for the end zone until we get to the forty or until it is fourth down."
- "We're going to be running, so save the time-out for the field goal. If it is fourth down or if a moving clock shows less than twenty-five, twenty-four, you don't have another play, so bleed the time before calling time-out." (The bleed, he knows, is down to 00:04.)
- "We're within field-goal range without a time-out. Be ready for your last play to be on first or second down, then your spike, then your kick. Or, your last to be on third down, then your hurry-on, then your kick."

Computing the Average Gain that You Need

To figure the average gain that you need per play, do the following:

Allow 15 seconds per play, which is an average of 10 for clock-stopping plays and 20 for others.

Divide the time-remaining by 15 to get the number of plays that you can run:

$$\frac{\text{time-remaining}}{15} = \text{number of plays}$$

Add one play for each time-out.

Divide the yards-to-go by the number of plays to get the average gain that you need per play:

$$\frac{\text{yards-to-go}}{\text{number of plays}} = \text{average needed per play}$$

If you see 01:05 and have three time-outs and the ball is on your 38, you mentally divide 65 (seconds) by 15 (seconds per play) and get a little over 4 plays; then you add 3 plays for 3 time-outs and divide 7 into 62 (yards to go) and get about 9. This calls for out routes or hooks or the like.

How fast can you do this "clock math"? Try it:

> You have 01:27 and two time-outs. The ball is on your 44, so there are 56 yards to go.
>
> That is 8 (6 + 2) into 56 for 7 yards per play.

Practice a few times, with varying numbers, and you will be doing this in two or three seconds.

Case: Oklahoma State vs. Texas A&M, second quarter. OSU gets the ball on the A&M 45, with 01:10 and two time-outs. The objective is simple: Try to get a TD but settle for a FG, call plays to get the chunks of yardage needed, keep stopping the clock, save the last time-out to get FG personnel on only if within FG range and expecting to be running on the play that would precede the FG, and make sure that the final play gets the ball into the end zone. The development is disappointing: OSU (a) loses seconds calling a time-out, (b) spikes away one of their last four downs after getting a first down on the 29 with 00:50, (c) passes with a 3rd-and-10, gains nine and one-half yards, and calls its last time-out, (d) kicks from too far away and misses. After the 1st-down spike, the booth misinforms us that OSU needs to save a time-out and, further, that they need the time-out to throw over the middle.

Imagining Yourself Talking to Your QB

You need a TD drive from your own 19, with 01:59 and three time-outs. You do the clock math—time for eight plays plus three for the time-outs, 81 yards to go, a little over seven yards per play—and you say to the QB: "We need a touchdown. Tell the guys we're playing fast. Use your time-outs the first three times you need to stop the clock. And remember your barriers for initiating clock-stopping or time-out plays—twenty-five, fifteen, and ten. Let's start by going for ten-yard chunks."

You need a TD and have 00:59 but no time-outs. The ball is on your 42, 2nd-and-six. You are talking to your QB during your final time-out. "We need a touchdown. We've got to throw. I will call only boundary and first-down passes. We cannot afford a sack or a single pass that does not get the clock stopped. We can get in six, maybe eight, plays."

Your defense is about to force a punt from inside your opponent's 10-yard line. You need a field goal to win. You will have two time-outs and about 01:12. You are talking to your QB. "We need a field goal. You are not to get sacked. If receivers are covered, throw the ball away. You know your throwaway points. Once we get to their twenty-five, any pass I call will be either the security pass or one of the quick passes. You call one time-out as soon as you need it. I will call the last one. If we don't have a time-out for the kick, remember that the spike is on third down or second and that the hurry-on is on fourth."

For more examples of talking to the QB see Appendix E.

9

Squeezing in Next-to-the-Last Plays

Squeezing in next-to-the-last plays is your most difficult job and the one with the most potential for getting you criticized.

Case: UCLA, in 1981, needs a FG to beat USC. They drive to the USC 33 and call their second time-out, at 00:28. They can run and get lined up to run again. If the QB sees that there will be 00:10 when the ball will be snapped, he can let the run go and use the last time-out. If he sees that there will be less, he can let the clock go down to 00:04 and call the time-out. But he gets off only one play, lets the clock move, calls time-out, and leaves the best field goal kicker in college football a little too far away. UCLA loses. No effort had been made to squeeze in a next-to-the-last play. The author was the offensive coordinator and QB coach.

Using the Word Penult

Something that is next-to-the-last is penultimate. The noun form of the word is penult. What you squeeze in is a penult. The word focuses attention on what you do in this most difficult job. It has no synonym.

Erecting Barriers To Prevent Mistakes

In stop-the-clock-offense the objective is to get the ball into the end zone before time expires in a second or a fourth quarter; it is to keep time from expiring before a final play or field-goal kick can be initiated.

If everything possible is going to be done before the final play, something must protect the final play. Something must ensure time to call it and initiate it. What does the protecting, the ensuring? Barriers—clock-time barriers that prevent you from trying kinds of plays for which you do not have time.

> ***Deciding on squeezing in next-to-the-last plays is the most difficult deciding that you do in managing the clock.***

There are three kinds of penults that need barriers. They are:

- boundary plays, end-zone passes, or time-out plays—plays that stop the clock until the snap,
- first-down passes that stop the clock at least temporarily, and
- regular plays that may leave the clock moving.

There are three kinds of clocks out of which these three kinds of penults can come. They are:

- stopped,
- temporarily-stopped, or first-down, and
- moving.

For each kind of clock there must be a minimum-number barrier for each kind of penult. For example, out of a stopped clock, the barrier below which you do not go with a play that will leave the clock stopped is 00:10.

With the kind of clock and the result of the kind of penult shown, the barriers are:

- stopped to stopped—00:10,
- stopped to temporarily-stopped—00:15,
- stopped to moving—00:30,
- temporarily-stopped to stopped—00:15,
- temporarily-stopped to temporarily-stopped—00:20,

- temporarily-stopped to moving—00:35,
- moving to stopped—00:30, 00:29,
- moving to temporarily-stopped—00:35, 00:34,
- moving to moving—00:45, 00:44.

For example, if a temporarily-stopped clock shows 00:17, you cannot use a first down pass that will only temporarily stop the clock. The barrier is 00:20. You can use a boundary pass that will stop the clock until the snap. The barrier for that is 00:15.

Case: Ohio State and Illinois are tied, 21-21. OSU starts on its own 10, with 03:40 and all three time-outs. They consume too much time and have a first down on the Illinois 22, with 00:21 and a time-out. There is plenty of time for one more run, the time-out, and the kick. Even 00:15 would be enough if the ballcarrier would not zig and zag. But they forgo a penult, let the clock go down to 00:06, call time-out, kick ... and win.

The barriers allow five extra seconds for initiating plays if the clock is not stopped until the snap.

For example, the barrier which you must not go beyond out of a temporarily-stopped clock, with a play that will leave the clock moving, is 00:35. That is five seconds to get started out of the temporarily stopped clock, 10 for the squeeze-in play, 15 to wait for substitutions, and a cushion of five because the clock is moving. You need to see 00:35 in order to execute a play and be able to initiate a final play.

The clock numbers are conservative. The barriers are meant to be safe. Why? Because

- both the execution of a play and the procedure of the umpire or the ref to get the ball ready and declare it ready can be slow, and
- fudging is best done from one side, and the safe side is the high side.

Here is an example of fudging:

Seeing 00:26, 00:25 on a moving clock at the end of a play means that you can execute a boundary play as a penult. (Seeing 00:31, 00:30 means that you can execute a first-down pass.) But your team is sharp, and the ref has been fast. Suddenly a play ends with 00:24, 00:23, and you call for a boundary play. You fudged down to 00:23. The QB gets ready to call for the snap, sees 00:08, 00:07, signals quickly for an end-zone pass, and calls for the snap at 00:03. You fudged too much, and he saved you.

Again, a barrier stops you—you cannot use a play that gets a certain kind of result if the clock time is less than that play's barrier time.

These barriers help most when they let you call a play that you want instead of a play that will just take a safe amount of time.

Case: Undefeated Georgia is trying, against Florida, to squeeze a TD into 36 seconds. They achieve a first down on their own 39 at 00:10. Time-outs are gone. It is barely possible to squeeze in a quick boundary pass and still launch an end-zone pass. They need 00:15, but can they fudge and try? What they do is spike, forgo a chance to have two passes, and ensure having one good pass.

Confronting the Barriers

In normal offense the play-caller has about 35 seconds between the time one play ends and the time another must begin. In stop-the-clock offense, if he does not want to lose time when the clock is either temporarily stopped for a first down or moving, he has only the 15 seconds that the officials take to get the ball ready. This means that he must be able to initiate the calling of the next play as the last play ends and, therefore, that he must anticipate before a play what he may need to call after the play.

It is the necessity to anticipate both the kinds of clocks and the barriers for the three kinds of penults that makes this so difficult. Anticipate you must, however, if you are to ensure that the final play will send the ball to the end zone and that the next-to-the-final play will contribute all it can.

> ***Clock-time barriers are to prevent you from attempting kinds of plays for which you do not have clock time.***

In this difficult phase, playing without a time-out, the play-caller calls a play and gets ready for one more play before the final one. But he does not know how much time will be left or whether the clock will be temporarily stopped or moving. (If the clock is stopped, he will have the 35 seconds, a luxury that is not being discussed here.) An example:

As his play ends, if the clock is temporarily stopped at 00:35, the play-caller will be able to call a regular play and still get off a final play. But if it is temporarily stopped at 00:25, he is going to have to call a first-down pass. If the clock is moving at 00:31, 00:30, he can call a boundary play. But if it is moving at 00:26, 00:25, he must forgo his penult and call for an end-zone pass. And, he must plan for these calls before that first play ends.

All of this means that, when he is trying to squeeze in a penult, he must have a picture in his mind of the barrier for whatever kind of play that penult is, and if the clock is below that barrier, he must go to the next kind of play and its barrier. Another example:

He wants to use a regular play as a penult and anticipates that he will have 00:45, 00:44, which is his barrier on a moving clock. But he sees 00:40, 00:39 as his immediate play ends. He is below his barrier. That means first-down pass, and he calls one without hesitation. If he had gotten a first down and seen 00:37, he could have used that regular play as the penult.

> *Squeezing requires anticipating two kinds of clocks—temporarily-stopped and moving—and barriers for plays that leave the clock stopped, temporarily stopped, and moving.*

Using the Barriers for Hurry-Ons and Spikes

The barriers advocated here can be used for hurry-ons and spikes. A hurry-on needs 20 seconds and, after a play, it can use the 15 allowed for the ref and the five allowed after the ready. For example:

> If you start with a clock stopped at 00:30, you have 10 seconds for a play, 15 for the ref, and five more to initiate the end-zone pass. The 15 plus the five is what you need for the hurry-on. The choice, then, is between a hurry-on and an end-zone pass. The choice does not include a boundary pass, for either it will be 4th down or time will be too short.

A spike can use the five seconds allowed for a final play, and a 1st- or 2nd-down/spike package can use the time allowed for a penult and a final play. A properly-executed spike will not, however, use all of the five seconds allowed for that final play. For example:

> Out of a temporarily-stopped clock, a play that will temporarily stop the clock plus a spike needs 00:20. That is 5 seconds to initiate the play, 10 to execute it, nothing for the ref, and 5 for the spike.

> **Case:** Florida gets a break before halftime—a first down on Miami's 41, with 00:26 and one time-out. A FG will tie it up. They get another first down at 00:13. The booth says, categorically, that they should spike. No. They can throw a quick boundary pass, then run straight at the goalposts, then call the time-out. What they do is throw for the end zone and get intercepted. Remember that a good QB, with 00:13 and possibly three snaps, does not want to spike away two seconds and have probably two snaps.

This is saying that, for simplicity, all three of the following efforts require approximately the same amount of time—00:21, 00:20 on a moving clock or 00:05 on a temporarily-stopped one:

> ***The barriers that protect final plays can be used to protect hurry-ons and spikes, spikes without the possibility of fudging.***

- a hurry-on and a kick,
- a spike and a final play,
- a final play.

Simplistic? Somewhat. You are asked to remember that there can be no fudging on a spike but that there can be on a hurry-on if it does not require too long a run to the ball-position.

Case: Louisville is losing to Kentucky, 0-16, in the second quarter. Louisville drives from its 20 to the Kentucky three and has 1st-and-goal, with 00:37. They throw for the end zone twice and have 00:28. Time-outs are gone. It is time for a run, but can they run and hurry on? Yes, although the ball is about as far away from the sideline as it can get. With a good decision they pass ... and score.

Using a Barrier for a Second FG Kick

FGs are usually 4th-down or last-down plays. To save time and a down for a second snap and then have a good first snap might be to give that time to your opponent for a kickoff return. The exception is in an extra period, when the clock is turned off.

Case: Georgia and Georgia Tech are tied in waning seconds. Tech kicks a FG on a 3rd down. It is blocked but recovered by a Tech player. Tech kicks a FG on 4th down, makes it, and demonstrates why some coaches advocate kicking on 3rd down when time is almost gone and the ball-position is good.

Mostly, if the snap for your kick is fumbled, your last play is a loudly-commanded, running pass with receivers fanning into the end zone. A 3rd-down spike after such a fumble is, by rule, not an option.

Avoiding Criticism

Why does this penult business have the most potential for criticism? If you attempt a penult and it allows time to expire, or if your final play fails when a good penult might have helped it succeed, you will find out. If you screw up and lose a game, you will find out. For more cases see Appendix F.

10

Using Up Excess Time before Scoring

At the end of either half, how do you both maximize your chances to score and limit your opponent's time to answer? Scoring is primary. Limiting his time is secondary.

Assessing the Problem

Here are questions that you face:

- With the time-outs that you have, how much time will you need in order to be able to use all four of your downs inside the 10?
- Do you have equally potent runs and passes? Can time-remaining, alone, dictate your calls? Or, do you need to favor either runs or passes in order to maximize your chance to score?
- How do you play outside the 10-yard line in order to have enough time, but not too much time, inside the 10?

When you are trying to score, you do not want to run out of time before you run out of downs.

Passing can risk stopping the clock and saving time for your opponent. Running can risk moving the clock and not leaving enough time for you.

A problem is that one weapon, be it a pass or a run, is going to be better than the other. A problem is that you will have about a 50-percent chance of either wanting to pass when there is excess time or wanting to run when there is limited time.

If you need a touchdown and can get it as surely by passing as by running and if running would consume the time you need to use all four downs inside the 10, you pass. If you can get the TD as surely by running as by passing and if passing might leave your opponent time after you use all four downs, you run.

The vagaries in time consumption are extreme: With a 1st-and-10 on your opponent's 12, you can pass for a TD and consume five seconds; or, you can do four methodical runs, get a 1st-and-goal, do four more, score on the fourth, and consume five minutes.

There is no point in trying to be precise. You cannot know when you will get a 1st-and-goal, where the ball will be, or on what down you might score.

Planning an Approach, Roughly

How can you plan in this indefiniteness? And, how can you be ready with an explanation of your plan if you score but do not consume excess time and your opponent scores and you lose? What can you do?

Five things:

1. Save all three time-outs for the end of a half. With three, you need to save about 35 seconds for a 1st-and-goal. With three, if you will throw one end-zone pass, you need to save only about 30 seconds. With none, you need to save about 95 seconds. The more time-outs you have, the fewer seconds you need to risk leaving for your opponent.
2. To adjust the speed of play, give hand-signals. The QB is the only player who needs to know of the adjusting.
3. Call plays as you do in stop-the-clock offense when you are worried about having all four of your plays, or, as you do in move-the-clock offense when you are worried about having excess time.
4. Have estimates for consumption. Given the indefiniteness, 30-second blocks work. Four unhurried runs need approximately four blocks or 02:00; three need three or 01:30; two need two or 01:00; one needs one or 00:30. For simplicity a whole block might be taken out for a play for which you have a

> *Maximizing your chances to score is primary.*
> *Limiting his time to answer is secondary.*

time-out. Three time-outs would then leave you needing 00:30. Also for simplicity a whole block might even be taken out for the anticipation of a pass play.

5. With your estimates, you want to be a little on the high side, so you will not be surprised by using up your time before you have used up your downs.

Have a clock-management specialist referring to numbers and telling you, "excess time," "you can run," "you must pass," and the like. Always, your questions are, "I know I can pass, but can I run?" and, "I know I can run, but can I afford to pass?"

What is the most time you might consume inside the 10? Figuring 10 seconds for a play and 35 between the ends of plays, about 02:45.

What is the least time you can use inside the 10? Playing FAST, using three time-outs, and having one incomplete pass, about 00:16 seconds. Let us say 00:20. Using two time-outs, 00:40; one, 01:00; none, 01:20.

Between the 20-yard line and the 10, allow for 30 seconds per play and for three plays, with one play being an incomplete pass. Allow, then, about 1:30.

Consuming Excess Time before Kicking for a Field Goal

Case: Georgia, behind by one with 05:38 left in a game against Alabama, punts from the +46. Penalty. They punt again from the -49. The ball goes to the 13. Alabama, after unnecessarily going out-of-bounds on 3rd down, has to punt. Georgia starts on the +34, with 03:45. Alabama has two time-outs. Georgia bleeds 46, 47, and 45 seconds with non-first-down runs and 28 with a first-down run. Alabama uses its time-outs at 00:47 and 00:42. Georgia sneaks on 3rd down to keep good lateral position. Their 4th-down kick is good. Alabama has 00:38 but gets intercepted. Great clockwork by Georgia! Consuming time can be exciting, too.

Usually, inside the 20, you want to run to avoid the risk of losing a field-goal opportunity to a holding penalty, a sack, or an interception. Usually, the problem of consuming excess time is easier, because you do not want to pass.

If you are positioning for a short field goal and are forced to kick on a 3rd down, nothing is lost. When your objective is to try for a touchdown but to settle for a field goal, you simply go for a TD with allowance for your concern about the dangers—sack, holding, interception.

> **Getting a TD from his 12 can take one play or eight plays and consume five seconds or one-third of a quarter.**

When consuming time in going for an easy field goal, with a one-point lead, you anticipate that your opponent might try to get you to score so he will have a chance to answer with eight points and get you into overtime.

You go for the field-goal line with the combination of plays that has the best percentage chance to get you there. If you have runs and passes that are interchangeable in their percentage chances and if your next first down will put you beyond the line, you can do what you do in going for a touchdown and try to arrive at your destination with the time almost gone.

Case: In the 2002 Super Bowl the St. Louis Rams got a 4th-quarter TD to tie but left the New England Patriots with enough time to get a FG to win. Should the Rams have left them with less time? No. They had to get that TD. With no time-outs, they were going to need time inside the 10 to execute four plays. Playing from behind, they did not want time to expire before they had used all four of their downs.

Case: It is 14-14, Texas and Kansas State, 4th quarter. Texas gets the ball on its 36, with 04:26. They want to score but leave KSU no time to answer. Texas gets to the +17 with 03:15. They run. They run again. Tension mounts. Someone in the booth is talking about turf toe. On 3rd-and-3 they throw, incomplete. Mistake. KSU is going to use the 40 seconds Texas did not use. A FG is good. KSU has 01:23. At 00:56, after a KSU first down on about the 50, the booth: "Now get up to the line and spike it." With 25 yards to gain and the clock stopped until the ready, spike it? No way. With 00:06 they kick from the +20 for the tie. It is blocked. Texas wins.

Counting on the QB to Bleed Seconds

One of the QB's difficult jobs is bleeding off the last few seconds before

- calling a time-out at 00:04, 00:03 after seeing 00:08, 00:07 or less, which is too little for a penult and a time-out,

- calling for the snap at 00:06 for a spike before a field-goal attempt, or
- calling for the snap at 00:04, 00:03 for a 4th-down play.

Case: Tennessee is losing to Memphis 16-17 in the fourth quarter. They have the ball on their 47, with 02:44 and one time-out. They run three times and are on the Memphis 41, with 01:27. Any excess time is gone. They start a run at 01:22, gain three, and call time-out at 01:01, wasting 15 seconds. They pass, pass again, pass again, pass again, and pass again. After getting a first down on the +17 at 00:20, they spike at 00:18, kick, and win. It was an effective drive, but they wasted time and, by not bleeding before the spike, left Memphis with time for a kickoff return and a play.

> ***If passes and runs were to have equal percentage chances to gain given yardages, decisions on using up excess time would not be difficult.***

Counting on the Holder to Bleed Seconds

Ideally, the holder is a QB who can watch the clock and signal for the snap the way he does when he is behind the center.

Whoever he is, he must be able to talk and keep his team steady while he waits for 00:04, 00:03 to signal for the snap.

Kicking on 3rd down with more than seven or eight seconds, when you want a down and time for a second kick, means you will risk saving your opponent time for a kickoff return. Do you want to take that risk? No.

Anticipating Your Opponent's Use of Time-Outs

Will your opponent use a time-out before you score? If you need only a field goal and are inside the 10 in front of the goalposts, yes, he will. If you are going to have enough time to use all four of your downs inside of the 10, no matter what he does, yes, he will. If you are not going to have time to use all of your downs, no, he will not.

11

Letting Your Opponent Score a TD

You let your opponent score a TD

- when it is the surest way to win,
- when you are down by one and your opponent can bleed the remaining seconds without making a first down, when he has yet to realize that he had better not score a TD to go up by eight and leave you time to answer, make a two-pointer, tie, and win in overtime,
- when you are tied and your opponent is close to your goal line and can bleed the remaining seconds before an almost certain field goal, when you see a better chance in giving him a TD, answering with a TD, kicking an extra point, and winning in overtime than you see in blocking his field goal or having him miss it,
- when you are ahead by one or two and your opponent is bleeding seconds and positioning for an almost certain field goal, when you like your chances of giving him a TD and answering with a winning TD better than you like your chances of having him not get the field goal, or
- when you just know that you are going to lose if you do not take drastic action.

You do not let him score a TD if you are behind by two or ahead by three. You make him protect his kicker and split the uprights. Your minus two would become minus nine, and your plus three could only be tied by his field goal.

> *You let your opponent score a TD when it is the surest way to win.*

Case: Maryland and North Carolina State are tied 21-21. Maryland has a first down on the NC State 16, with 01:39. Maryland runs for three, to the 13. NC State uses its second time-out, trying to save time for an answer. Should NC State let Maryland score and have time left for a seven-point answer and a chance to win in overtime? Are they certain to lose if they do not? They do not. Maryland kicks. They lose.

Deciding

Deciding is difficult. Why? Four reasons:

1. Each of the three operative differentials—minus one, zero, and plus one or plus two—leaves you with a different need.
2. Your time-remaining and time-outs are huge factors.
3. Percentage chances of different things getting done—a kick being blocked or missed, driving 60 yards for a FG, driving 80 yards for a TD, making a two-pointer, winning in overtime—must be weighed.
4. The possibility of the opponent taking a knee and precluding your tactic must be anticipated.

What you do not want to do in a tie is let your opponent score a TD and leave you in need of a TD, when you could have yielded the FG and had time left over to answer with a tying FG.

What you must weigh in your mind is the chance of (a) preventing a FG, against the chance of (b) driving for a score. If you have a 2% chance of doing (a) and a 10% chance of doing (b), you have to go with (b).

Allowing Time to Answer

You let him score when it is 1st-and-goal. The problem is estimating how much time, if any, would be left for you after his 4th-down FG. If there would not be enough for your necessary answer, you want to consider going ahead and letting him score.

Figuring conservatively, let us say that you would need, after your opponent's FG,

- four plays to get a FG and
- eight plays to get a TD.

If you would not have time for these plays, after his FG, you want to consider letting him score.

The following numbers assume that (a) your opponent is going for a FG, (b) he is trying to consume time so you cannot answer, (c) he is driving, and his 1st-and-goal stops the clock only temporarily, (d) you have no time-outs, and (e) your FG answer, at 10 seconds per clock-stopping play, would require 40 seconds and your TD answer, 70.

The numbers by which he can bleed the time are made up of

- 5 for a play for which you have a time-out,
- 25 for the 25-second counter and a 1st-down play, and
- 45 for the ref, the counter, and a play.

This means that you apply a 25 for his first play and either 5s or 45s for his other three, get a sum, subtract the sum from the clock time, and get the amount of time you would have, if any, after his 4th-down play or kick.

This card is for a clock-management specialist:

Times He Can Take to Get a 4th-Down FG

Your Time-Outs

Downs	3	2	1	0
1st	00:40	01:20	02:00	02:40
2nd	00:15	00:55	01:35	02:15
3rd		00:10	00:50	01:30
4th			00:05	0:45

The card says that, if it is a 2nd down and you have one time-out, your opponent will consume 01:35 getting his FG. You subtract this from what is on the clock to know what you would have left after his FG. To know what you would have if you were to let him score, you simply note what is on the clock.

If you are counting from a change of possession, you must subtract 20 seconds from the time you predict he will take.

What if he starts on your 12, and you use your time-outs to save yourself some time, and then he gets a 1st-and-goal on your two? The possibility cannot be avoided. Football is full of gambles.

Times for an Opponent's FG and Your 60-Second TD Answer

Your Time-Outs

Downs	3	2	1	0
1st	01:40	02:20	03:00	03:40
2nd	01:15	01:55	02:35	03:15
3rd		01:10	01:50	02:30
4th			01:05	01:45

If less than shown, you should let him score. Times for his FG and your 30-second FG drive would be these times minus 30. What you do not want to do, with a one- or a two-point lead, is let your opponent score a TD when you could have yielded the FG and had time to answer with a winning FG.

Being Down by One

If there would be some time left after his FG, you must compare

- letting him execute his plays and kick the FG and, then, answering with a winning TD in the limited time, and
- letting him score and, then, answering with a TD and a two-pointer and a victory in overtime.

These possibilities are difficult to compare. What you have to do, mainly, is establish an amount of time that you would need to score and, with that established, either yield to the FG if it would leave you that much time or let the opponent score if it would not. If you are considering waiting for him to kick a FG, it should mean that you would have time to score if he were to get the FG.

> ***Your decision to let your opponent score needs to be when it is 1st-and-goal and his FG is a near certainty.***

Being Tied

In a tie, an opponent will kick. Now you must ask:

- If he *can* bleed all of the remaining time before kicking, can you block the kick or make him miss it and get to overtime? Or, should you let him score, save some time, and try for a TD and new life in overtime?

- If he *cannot* bleed all of the time, can you take what he leaves you after his FG, drive for your FG, and get to overtime? Or, should you let him score and have more time but the need for a TD.

Being Ahead By One Or Two

The question is the same, whether ahead by one or two: How much time would you have left after his go-ahead 4th-down FG. If you would have enough, you would need only a FG to win. If you would not have enough and would let him score a TD on his 1st down, you would need a TD to win.

> **Case:** Purdue, down by two to Michigan, is on the +10, with 02:17 left in the game. Then: illegal procedure, a formation problem, a mistake in dealing with a blitz, and a missed FG. Pressure! To make matters worse, Purdue could have had two extra points earlier when they tried two two-pointers and failed with both. Michigan gets the ball and has a 3rd-and-11 on their own 19. Should they throw and risk stopping the clock or should they run with less chance of making it but with the certainty of consuming 40 seconds? They throw, miss, and punt to the Purdue 40. Now 01:41 remains. Purdue gets a first down on the 21. Purdue's QB spikes. Booth: "It was to catch Michigan with 12 men on the field." Later, it is 1st-and-five on the 16, with 00:44. Should Michigan let them have a TD and try to answer with a TD? If they do not, they are going to get beat. But, Purdue has a rattled FG kicker. Also, the ball is beyond the 10. Michigan takes a time-out at 00:23. The Purdue QB runs the ball to the middle, lets the clock go down to 00:08, and spikes, unnecessarily leaving Michigan time for a kickoff return. Purdue kicks. Good! The kickoff return, with a long lateral pass, fails. Purdue wins.

> ***There can be a time when intentionally giving up a lead can improve your chances of winning.***

Using Clock Offense in a Wind

In a wind, near a change of quarters, you want either to keep or to put the wind behind you in case you have to punt or want to kick a field goal.

Deciding What to Do

- **With the wind, as you try to make a first down,** you do stop-the-clock offense—pass and run wide to get out-of-bounds.

- **Against it**, you do move-the-clock offense—run but stay inbounds.

- **With it,** you figure safely—15 seconds for the ref, 10 for the play.

- **Against it,** you figure safely—10 seconds for the ref, 5 for the play.

- **With it,** you do not let yourself run out of time you counted on having.

- **Against it,** you use up all the time you can.

- **With it,** the question is, Can I run and risk using up too much time?

- **Against it,** Can I pass and risk not using up enough time?

Facing the Difficulty in Deciding

Decisions can be very difficult.

- **With the wind,** there can be 3rd-and-inches with 00:14 showing and, if you run and fail to gain, you will have to either (a) burn a time-out or (b) change ends and punt or kick into the wind.
- **Against it,** there can be 3rd-and-eight with 00:14 showing and, if you pass and it is incomplete, you will have to punt or kick into the wind.
- **With it,** there can be 3rd-and-inches with 00:14 and, if you pass incomplete, you will still get to punt or kick with the wind.
- **Against it,** there can be 3rd-and-eight with 00:14 and, if you run and fail, you will either be (a) punting or kicking with the wind or (b) forcing your opponent to burn a time-out.

Inevitably, you are going to be in wind and trying to determine what you can do and still have the wind for a punt or FG kick. Inevitably, you are going to want someone looking at your prepared numbers and advising you.

> *With the wind, your time-outs are a factor;*
> *against the wind, your opponent's are.*

Applying Prepared Numbers

The two tables in this chapter show the downs and whether you can run with the wind or pass against it, for the first-down line, thrice, twice, or once when you see at least the times shown for clocks that are moving, temporarily stopped, and stopped.

The numbers in the with-the-wind table, which show as plays end, allow

- 15 for the ref,
- 5 from the 25-second counter,
- 10 for a play, clock stopped,
- 15 (5 and 10) for a HUSTLE play, clock temporarily stopped,
- 30 (15, 5, and 10) for a HUSTLE play, clock moving, and
- 25 for either a hurry-on punt or a hurry-on field goal, after a 3rd-down run.

	You Can Run with the Wind, without a Time-Out		
1st Down	moving	temporarily stopped	stopped
thrice	xxx	01:40	01:35
twice	xxx	01:20	01:15
once	xxx	01:00	00:55
2nd Down			
twice		01:25	01:05
once		01:05	00:45
3rd Down			
once		00:55	00:35

The number of 01:40, for running thrice out of a temporarily-stopped clock before a 1st-down play, is built this way:

   5 from the counter
  10 for the first play
  60 for the second and third plays
  25 for the hurry-on punt or kick, after a 3rd-down run
 ___
 100 seconds or 01:40

The number of 01:20 for running twice and passing incomplete once, out of a temporarily-stopped clock before a 1st-down play, has a 10-second pass replacing a 30-second run.

The numbers in the against-the-wind table allow

   10 for the ref,
   20 more from the counter,
    5 for a play,
   25 (20 and 5) for a play, clock temporarily stopped,
   35 (10, 20, and 5) for a play, clock moving,
   30 (10 and 20) for a 4th down to let the quarter end.

Against the wind, your time-outs are not a factor. Your opponent's are, although you cannot plan on his using them.

You Can Pass against the Wind, without an Opponent's Time-Out			
1st Down		temporarily	
	moving	stopped	stopped
thrice	xxx	00:35	00:15
twice	xxx	01:05	00:45
once	xxx	01:35	01:15
2nd Down			
twice	00:40		00:10
once	01:10		00:40
3rd Down			
once	00:35		00:05

The number of 01:35 for passing once out of a temporarily-stopped clock, before a first-down play, is built this way:

    20 for the counter, since there is no change of possession
      5 for the incomplete 1st-down pass
      5 for the 2nd-down play
    35 for up to and including the 3rd-down play
    30 for the 4th-down to let the quarter end
    95 or 01:35

For purposes of punting or kicking with the wind, the numbers in the two tables answer the questions, Can you run, fail, and not have the quarter end? and, Can you pass, fail, and still have the quarter end?

Practicing in Simulation

Practicing in simulation involves an assistant giving the clock-management specialist situations—down, distance, wind, and time—and having the specialist refer to his numbers and give the play-caller advice, such as:

- "You can run once more or pass at least twice."
- "You can pass twice."

> *In no aspect of clock management is there any substitute for practicing decision-making indoors in simulation.*

Anticipating the Fourth Quarter

At the coin-toss, if there is a strong north or south wind that is expected to continue and if you want the wind in the fourth quarter in case there is clock offense and if you win the toss, you should take the ball; then, count on your opponent taking the ball in the third quarter, so you can get the wind in the fourth. If you lose the toss and he defers, you should take the ball; then, count on him taking the ball in the third, so you can get the wind in the fourth.

It would be difficult for him to give you the ball to start both halves.

Assessing the Difficulty of Deciding

This aspect of clock management is about

- knowing the percentage chances that your plays have of making the various yardages and being able to hold those percentage chances in your mind as you look at the eventualities that will result from failure,
- knowing, for example, that a pass has a 60 percent chance and a run a 30 percent chance of making six yards into a wind and, then, weighing those percentages against the probability of a failed pass leaving you punting or kicking into the wind and a failed run leaving you punting or kicking with the wind.

It is about working between pressures. You will confront dilemmic choices. You must practice through them in simulation until you can keep from being nonplussed when the better choice is not clearly distinguishable.

> **It all boils down to:**
> **Can you run, fail, and not have the quarter end?**
> **And, can you pass, fail, and still have the quarter end?**

13

Deciding on Kicking a FG or Going for a TD

Facing the Difficulty

On a 4th down you have three points if you want to take them. Do you give up the three for a try at seven? How do you weigh the seven, if failing to get them will mean succeeding in getting good field position for your defense?

Mostly, when you expect more scoring, you kick. Exceptions are at those differentials where seven or eight points will take you from being behind to tying or being ahead. Those are –4, –5, –6, –7, and –8. Mostly, though, three points leaves you needing significantly less or him needing significantly more.

Case: Southern California is ahead of California 27-21 in the fourth quarter. They have 4th-and-goal inside the one, with 01:45. Cal is out of time-outs. Should USC run and, at worst, make Cal go 99 yards with no time-outs, or should they kick to go up by nine but risk a block, a scoop, and a score or risk a kickoff return and a drive? USC kicks, goes up by nine, yields a TD, fields the onside kick, and wins 30-28.

Clock management encompasses all phases of the kicking game.

Glance at what three points does to a tie or a lead:

0 + 3 = 3	4 + 3 = 7	8 + 3 = 11
1 + 3 = 4	5 + 3 = 8	9 + 3 = 12
2 + 3 = 5	6 + 3 = 9	10 + 3 = 13
3 + 3 = 6	7 + 3 = 10	11 + 3 = 14

From every differential, adding three leaves you significantly better off.

Glance next at what three does to a deficit:

-1 + 3 = +2	-5 + 3 = -2	-9 + 3 = -6
-2 + 3 = +1	-6 + 3 = -3	-10 + 3 = -7
-3 + 3 = 0	-7 + 3 = -4	-11 + 3 = -8
-4 + 3 = -1	-8 + 3 = -5	-12 + 3 = -9

Again, you are significantly better off, although from -4 through -9, the field goal leaves you behind, where a touchdown would have given you a chance to tie or go ahead.

A further reason to kick is to give your offense a better chance to end a drive with an accomplishment.

Even though you mostly kick, the decisions that you must make can be difficult. Your choices are just three—FG, first down, or TD—but they can be influenced by a host of factors:

- the scoring needed by the team that is behind,
- the possibilities of succeeding with each of the three choices,
- the resulting field-positions that go with failures,
- your defense,
- your punt return,
- your kick-off coverage,
- your onside-kick coverage,
- the weather,
- your two-point play proficiency,
- your feeling about playing in an extra period, and
- your team's psychological state.

> **Each point differential gives you a different comparison of (a) +3 and (b) either +7 or, if you turn the ball over, 0, with your defense in good field position.**

When the clock becomes a factor, choices are further influence by:
- time-remaining and
- time outs.

For one example of how a variation in one influencing factor can affect a decision, imagine this situation:
- differential, -6
- LOS, +15
- lateral ball-position, middle
- time-outs, two
- time-remaining, 02:30
- 1st-and-10

Now, put a down-and-distance of 4th-and-4 with it. Go for a first down? Probably. Making four yards and going on for a TD is probably easier than making a FG, kicking off, holding him, driving for another FG, and winning in an extra period. Next, put 4th-and-9 with it. Does that make you want to kick and stay alive. Possibly.

For another example, imagine:
- differential, -6
- LOS, +5
- lateral position, right hash for a right-footed kicker
- time-outs, two
- time remaining, 02:30

Now, put 4th-and-3 with it. The kick is difficult. Go for a TD? Probably.

Now, put the ball in the middle. Kick? Possibly.

In short, these factors, which can be considered only in your gut, influence choices.

Allowing for Time-Remaining

If you are behind, a step to take before considering time and time-outs is to get an assessment of what you need. Possibilities to tie or win are:

- a FG, = 3
- two FGs, = 6
- a TD, = 6 (7)
- a TD and a 2-pointer, = 8
- a TD and a FG, or = 6(7), 9(10)
- a TD, a 2-pointer, and FG. = 11

If you are ahead, mostly, you kick. Unless the kick is difficult and the first down much less difficult, or unless the TD is not difficult at all, you kick

Your opponent's driving and scoring would take about the same amount of time after a successul FG effort by you as it would after an unsuccessful TD effort by you. Therefore, his time is not a factor in deciding between a kick or a play. Your time is. You do not count on a second score that you do not have time to get.

The choice that is difficult comes when you are behind by 4, 5, 6, 7, or 8. The choice is between

- taking an easy FG, getting within range to win, kicking off and stopping him, taking his punt, and driving for a win with whatever points are needed,

and

- trying for a first down or a TD, maybe going on to win or tie, maybe failing, turning the ball over, having to stop him, taking his punt, and driving for a win or a tie.

At these point differentials, if there is less time than the amount needed for a FG and the necessary drive, you want to go ahead and try to get a TD.

What is the amount needed, assuming that you can keep your opponent from making a first down once he starts back at you? If you figure that he will average 10 seconds for plays for which you have time-outs and 40 for others and that you will average 15 seconds per play while driving 80 yards in 10-yard chunks, the amount is between three minutes if you have three time-outs, and four minutes and 15 seconds if you have none.

The four minutes and 15 seconds, assuming no time outs, is built this way:

  10 for your FG

  10 for your kickoff

   0 before his first play

120 for his three plays

  10 for his punt

105 for seven plays from your 20

255 ~~minutes~~ seconds or 04:15

This estimating is rough, but with so many unpredictabilities, rough has to do.

Comparing the Alternative Approaches

It can be difficult to fix in your mind what it is that you must compare. For example, you are down by eight, it is 4th-and-four on his 12, you have one time-out, and you must compare:

- kicking and making it minus five,
- kicking off and stopping him,
- taking his punt,
- driving for a TD to win

with

- making a TD and a two-pointer,
- kicking off and stopping him,
- playing in overtime

or

- failing to make a TD,
- stopping him and taking his punt,
- driving for a TD and making a two-pointer, and
- playing in overtime.

Again, time-remaining is a factor when you are considering taking a FG even though it would require that you have time to drive for another score. And, in this consideration, a card can help.

Following is a card for a clock-management specialist to refer to:

Time Needed to Kick a FG, Kickoff, Stop Your Opponent, and Drive				
Time-outs	3	2	1	0
For a FG	02:30	03:00	03:30	04:00
For a TD	03:00	03:30	04:00	04:30

The 03:00 for driving for a FG with two time-outs is built this way:

```
 10  for your FG
 10  for your kickoff
 60  for his three plays (10, 10, and 40)
 10  for his punt
 90  for your six plays from your 20
  0  for your FG
─────
180  or 03:00
```

95

Practicing in Simultation

For your practice you want the assisting coach to move the ball and guide the stop-watch operator into situations where you will have to make difficult decisions.

At one exteme the assistant might present an eight-point deficit, a sure FG, a difficult first down, a difficult TD, three time-outs, a good defense, and 04:00. This situation would invite a FG.

At another extreme he might present the same deficit but a difficult FG, a 4th-and-inches, one time-out, a tired defense, and 02:00. This would invite a run for the first down. Failing with the run would require stopping your opponent, taking his punt, driving for a TD, and adding a two-pointer, all in less than two minutes.

Practicing must be making not only good decisions but unhesitating ones. The difficulty in doing this will go unnoticed by all fans and most radio and TV commentators, but it must not go unsimulated by you. Skip practicing and you risk letting your players down.

Case: In a national championship game, Florida State is down 0-3 to Oklahoma and has a 4th-and-one on Oklahoma's 19, with about 07:00 left. They kick, miss, and lose. With 07:00 left, should they have tried to get a first down and a TD? Some coaches would say yes; some, no.

Case: Penn State needs nine points to tie Minnesota and has 4th-and-six on the +29, with 01:02. Should they kick and hope to get within a TD of winning, or should they go for a first down and hope to score a TD and get within a FG of winning? Either way they must recover an onside kick. The decision is a tough one. They go for the first down, fail, and lose.

Case: Ahead by seven, Oklahoma has a 4th-and-three on the Kansas State 29, with 01:28 on a stopped clock. The national championship is on the line. The dilemma: (1) Go for the three yards to end the game, but risk giving KSU the ball, or (2) kick to end the game, but risk a blocked kick, a scoop, a KSU touchdown, and an extra period. Oklahoma kicks, makes it, and goes on to win the national championship.

14

Deciding on Punting or Going for a First Down

Case: Southern Mississippi scores to get within five of East Carolina, 9-14. An onside kick fails. ECU proceeds to consume time, and they get to a 4th-and-very-short on the USM 36, with 01:53. Should they punt or go for it? Someone in the booth says they must go for it. Someone else suggests the possibility of taking a knee. A knee? What ECU does is let the 25-second counter run out, take a delay penalty, and punt out-of-bounds, which is risky because a punt to a side is easier to block. USM tries to answer but cannot. ECU wins. It was a watershed decision, where some coaches would have gone one way and some the other.

Deciding through the Game

Deciding usually has nothing to do with clock time and time-outs. You have a 4th down around his 35, and you weigh the possibilities of

- making the first down and, maybe, going on to score,
- failing to make it and giving your opponent good field position,
- punting and leaving him on his 20,
- punting and, maybe, leaving him inside his 20, and
- having a punt go awry.

You adjust the yard line at which you will go for it—that is the line that establishes four-down territory—according to

- the distance to gain, and
- the degree to which you must gamble in order to win.

Following is an example of a basic adjustment plan for yard lines and distances-to-gain. It says that you go for a first down from his 35 if it is 4th-and-four, five, or six but that you adjust the yard line for distances-to-gain that are shorter and longer:

Go for It Rather than Punt, Generally

4th-and-one	38	4th-and-six	35
4th-and-two	37	4th-and-seven	34
4th-and-three	36	4th-and-eight	33
4th-and-four	35	4th-and-nine	32
4th-and-five	35		

It helps to have in mind the yard line you need to be on in order to go for it with the middle distances of four, five, and six. With the line established, you can move it closer to the goal line for the longer distances-to-go and farther away for the shorter.

> **Do you punt or do you risk failing with a play and giving your opponent good field position? That is the question.**

Deciding when Time is Short

Deciding can, however, have everything to do with clock time and time-outs. If you are

- ahead by one score, can you go for a first down to avoid the risks of punting and, if you fail to make it, can you hold your opponent until time expires, or, should you punt?
- behind by one score, can you punt, hold him, get the ball back, and have time to score the points you need, or, should you go for it?

Deciding when You are Ahead

Case: Tennessee scores on Georgia to get to within five, 13-18, with 03:21 to go in the fourth quarter. Tennessee has one time-out. Georgia has three. The onside kick fails, and Georgia has the ball, with 03:17. A few plays later it is 3rd-and-two just inside Tennessee territory. Georgia's 3rd-down play, at 01:52, fails. Should they run, with 4th-and-one? Or, should they pooch punt? It is a watershed decision. Georgia runs, makes it, bleeds time, and celebrates.

Most of the time, you decide as you decide throughout a game. However, in a situation where you would ordinarily punt, what if going for it and failing would leave your opponent with time for only one play? Would you rather (a) protect your punter, probably against an 11-man rush, or (b) possibly play defense for one play from poor field position?

Your questions are:

- where is the ball?
- how far do you have to go?
- how good is your punting game? and
- how many plays can your opponent execute if you go for it and fail?

Let us say that, with the ball, he would gain 10 yards per play with a time expenditure of 5 seconds before his first play and 10 seconds per play. This would be with the clock stopping for incompletes, first downs, out-of-bounds balls, and time-outs. With these assumptions and with a field-goal line at the 25, it would take him these times from these yard lines to get FGs and TDs:

Times for His Scores, after Your 4th-Down Failures		
your yard line	times for his FG	times for his TD
+ 35	00:45	01:15
+ 45	00:35	01:05
− 45	00:25	00:55
− 35	00:15	00:45

The time numbers are low, which is the safe way to have them when you are giving up your chance to punt because you feel protected by the clock.

Again, if you decide not to punt, you are saying that you are going to avoid risking a blocked punt by risking playing defense from wherever you are for whatever estimate you make of the number of plays he can execute.

Deciding when You are Behind

To punt is to assume that you can hold your opponent and get a return punt. Always, you consider the yard line and the distance-to-go. Now, in addition, you consider

- how much time will he consume with three plays, and
- how much time will you need after taking his return punt.

> ***You want to have practiced making decisions
> so you will make them unhesitatingly.***

Presumably, if you are not going to have enough time, you will go for the first down. To be safe in anticipating your opponent's consumption, allow 10 seconds for your punt, zero seconds before his 1st-down play, 10 seconds for every play for which you have a time-out, 40 for the others, and 10 for his punt. You are counting on the time that will be left, so you do not want him consuming more than you allowed for.

Since you do not know where his punt will leave you, let us just estimate that you will need 01:30 to get a TD, enough to give you six plays from your own 40, and 01:00 to get a FG, enough to give you four plays.

Following is an example of what can be on a card:

Deciding If You Can Punt, Get the Ball Back, and Drive				
Your time-outs	3	2	1	0
For a TD				
times to get ball back	00:50	01:20	01:50	02:20
times to drive for TD	01:30	01:30	01:30	01:30
total needed	02:20	02:50	03:20	03:50
For a FG				
time to get ball back	00:50	01:20	01:50	02:20
times to drive for FG	01:00	01:00	01:00	01:00
total needed	01:50	02:20	02:50	03:20

In the bottom right-hand corner, the 03:20 says that, if there is 03:20 on the clock, you should have enough time to punt, get the ball back, and drive for a FG.

Your times may be different but, whatever they are, if you have fewer seconds on the clock than you have on your card, you will presumably go for the first down.

Making the Decision

It can be easy.

- You are on the opponent's 40, ahead by nine, with 4th-and-10 and 02:00. Your opponent has three time-outs. You have a good punter for this position.

    Decision: Punt. Make him work. Do not risk giving the opponent momentum by giving him the ball on his 40.

Or, it can be wrenching.

- You are on your own 35, behind by two, with 4th and four and 02:59. You have one time-out. You have a good punting game. If you punt, all your opponent needs is one first down.

    Decision: Would you have a better chance of making four yards now and going on to score than you would have of punting, stopping him in three downs, and getting the three points before time is up? Some coaches would go for it; some would punt.

Generally, favor

- punting if you are ahead and are some distance from his goal line, and
- going for it if you are behind and are not too far from his goal line.

    Case: Notre Dame is behind Boston College by seven. BC has the ball. On a 4th-and-inches in ND territory they let the clock go down to 00:22, take a delay penalty, and punt. The punt gives ND two plays. Should BC have tried to run for six inches? ND would still have had a long way to go. Wrenching!

15

Deciding on an Extra Point in Final Seconds

Taking a Knee when There is No Time Left

At the end of a game, if you score and go ahead by +1 or +2 and leave no time on the clock, you do not kick for an extra point and give your opponent a chance to block the kick, scoop it up, score two points, and beat you or put you into overtime. You take a knee. There is no deciding.

If you score and go ahead by three or more or if you stay behind by three of more, the rule as of 2006 says, "during a down in which the fourth period expires, the try (for one or two points) shall not be attempted "because the point or points would not affect the outcome of the game."

Deciding when There is a Little Time Left

Deciding comes when you go ahead, there is a little time left, and you find yourself having to consider

- taking a knee and, then, stopping (a) a kickoff return, (b) a quickly-downed return and one snap, or (c) after a touchback, one snap from his 20,

> **After a score and after time has expired, you do not want to give your opponent any chance to beat you.**

- taking a knee and, then, stopping (a) a kickoff return, (b) a quickly-downed return and two snaps, or (c) after a touchback, two snaps,
- kicking and risking a block, a scoop, and a two-point score, while trying to protect yourself by going from +2 to +3, +3 to +4, +6 to +7, +7 to +8, +8 to +9—going to a score that will make it more difficult to beat you, or
- going for two and risking a fumble, a scoop, and a score, while trying to protect yourself by going from +1 to +3, +4 to +6, or +5 to +7, by going to a score that will make it more difficult to beat you.

Deciding involves consideration of time. When there is time left, the go-ahead differentials of +1, +4, and +5 separate from the others. At those you want to either take a knee or go for two because an extra point would not change what your opponent needs to beat you. On the other hand the block/scoop/score and the −2 would change his need—a +1 would become −1, a +4 a +2, and a +5 a +3. Now, do you take a knee or go for two? To go for two is to risk a stop, a takeaway, and a score. There is another separation: taking a knee does not risk a 2-point score by him, while going for two does; taking a knee will not get you protective points, while going for two can.

There is still another separation: going for two from a +1 differential can make it +3, while going for two from a +4 can make it only +6 and an identical need for him.

How do you think? There is more of a chance of a kickoff return than there is of the block, scoop, and score. So, you kick or go for two to get protective points. You get points that will help you, and you risk the block and the unlikely two-point score.

As of 2007 a kickoff-clock will start with the ball being controlled on the field of play.

Imagine that you do not want to risk giving your opponent time for two plays or for one play and a kick, that you would rather try a conversion; but, that you will risk his one play, that you would rather not try a conversion.

> **Do you try to score to protect yourself against a score, while giving him a chance to score? This is the question.**

For purposes of planning, then, imagine that 00:06 or less is not enough time for a field goal but is enough for a return, or a quickly-downed return and one snap, or one snap from his 20; that from 00:07 to 00:12 there is enough time for a long return and one snap, or two snaps; and that 00:13 or more is too much time for turning down a try for one or two and taking a knee, until the differential becomes +9, +10, or more.

For purposes of taking a knee this means that you

- will if there is 00:06 or less and you are ahead by 1, 2, 4, 9, or 10,
- will not if there is 00:07 to 00:12 and, excepting 4, you are ahead by 8 or less,
- will, however, if there is 00:13 or more and you are ahead by 4 or by 9 or more.

At the differentials of +9 and +10 you want to take a knee with any time that does not allow your opponent two scores. You do not want to risk the block/scoop/score or the fumble/scoop/score and him getting within 7 or 8.

Having a Card Ready

Figuring all of this during a game is not possible. Figuring it beforehand, having prepared decisions on a card, and having a clock-management specialist relay to you, "take a knee", "go for two", "kick", or the like, is possible. Following is an example of a card.

Deciding After Scoring In Final Seconds

Knee (Kn), Extra Point (XP), Two Points (Tw)

Point Differential

Time-remaining	+1	+2	+3	+4	+5	+6	+7	+8	+9	+10
00:00	Kn	Kn	Kn	Kn	Kn	Kn	Kn	Kn	Kn	Kn
00:01 to 00:06	Kn	Kn	XP	Kn	Tw	XP	XP	XP	Kn	Kn
00:07 to 00:12	Tw	XP	XP	Kn	Tw	XP	XP	XP	Kn	Kn
00:13 or more	Tw	XP	XP	Kn	Tw	XP	XP	XP	Kn	Kn

16

Trying for Two Points

Deciding when to Try

After scoring a touchdown, you have about a 33% chance of making three yards and getting two points and almost a 100% chance of kicking and getting one point. With three TDs, trying for twos should get you two points, while kicking for ones would surely get you three.

So, when do you try for two?

- You try for two when you can fail and not have failing affect the scoring needed by the team that is behind.
- You try for two when getting a sure one would make no difference in what the losing team would have to do to catch up and when the clock tells you that the losing team has time only to catch up.

If the ball is moved to the one and one-half yard line by a penalty, you have about a 67% chance of getting two. There is seldom a cumulative effect, however, because even one such penalty in a game is rare. You try for two from the one and one-half yard line with almost the same considerations that you try for two from the three.

Case: Duke scores on Wake Forest and is down 9-14, by 5, in the first quarter. The two-point-try card has 5 on it. They go for two, miss, and stay down by five. Near the end of the game they score and are down 25-28, by 3. If they had made a one-pointer earlier, they would be down by two and could try a two-pointer to get into overtime. Duke had gone for two too early.

Questioning Why Certain Differentials Are on the Card

The possibilities for failing on a two-point try and not living to regret not succeeding on a sure one-point try reside in these pairs of numbers:

- 1 and 2
- 4 and 5
- 5 and 6
- 12 and 13

These numbers, in their pairs, are the same for a team that is behind. To go from one number to the other does not change the scoring needed. If going for two points and failing leaves you with one number and if going for one would have taken you only to the other number, you will not pay a price for having passed up the chance to go for one. In other words, you do not need to kick to go from one number in a pair to the other.

Let examples from one pair make the point for all four pairs:

- You score and are behind by 13. If you make a one-pointer, you will be behind by 12 and no better off than if you try a two-pointer, fail, and stay behind by 13.
- You score and are ahead by 12. If you make a one-pointer, you will be ahead by 13 and no better off than if you try a two-pointer, fail, and stay ahead by 12.

On what is universally referred to as the "card", you have these numbers that tell you to go for two if you expect only the scoring needed by the team that is behind. In football scoring, these are the only differentials of their kind.

- +12, +5, +4, +1
- −13, −6, −5, −2

Case: McNeese State scores to get within 12 of Western Kentucky. From the booth: "Got to go for two." McNeese State goes for two and fails. Minus 12 is not on anyone's card. They needed to kick and keep alive their hopes of getting a FG, a TD, a two-pointer, and rebirth in an extra period.

> *You go for two when, because of the clock and possible scoring, getting one is no better than getting zero.*

Is it clear that, if you are considering only the scoring needed by the team that is behind, it makes little difference whether that team is left needing 2 rather than 1, 5 rather than 4, 6 rather than 5, or 13 rather than 12; that it makes little difference if you pass up a sure one-pointer and miss trying a two-pointer.

Case: Penn State is down by 15 to Minnesota, with five minutes left in the game. Needing two TDs, they cannot afford to let seconds slip away, but they huddle with the clock moving and, generally, do not husband time. They get a TD, go for two, fail, and leave themselves behind by nine points. It would have been more encouraging to their players to kick and leave themselves behind by eight points and one scoring drive.

Questioning Why Other Differentials Are not on the Card

In the remaining differentials there is a distinct advantage in making sure one-pointers. The first numbers—the numbers on the left in each column—are the differentials after touchdowns; the second have added valuable one-pointers. The second numbers are all significantly better than the first. The xxxx's are for where the first numbers would be the numbers on the card.

+15/+16	-16/-15
+14/+15	-15/-14
+13/+14	-14/-13
xxxx	xxxx
+11/+12	-12/-11
+10/+11	-11/-10
+9/+10	-10/-9
+8/+9	-9/-8
+7/+8	-8/-7
+6/+7	-7/-6
xxxx	xxxx
xxxx	xxxx
+3/+4	-4/-3
+2/+3	-3/-2
xxxx	xxxx
+0/+1	-1/-0

Let one example make this point that you go for two only when considering the scoring needed by the team that is behind: Your TD leaves you ahead by five points. Your card has on it +5. It is early in the third quarter. If you go for two and fail, your opponent still has to get a TD. But, if you fail and he scores 14, he will be ahead by nine, and you will wish you had kicked so he would be ahead by only eight.

Case: Virginia Tech scores a TD against Syracuse and is behind 9-14. There is a −5 on the card. It is in the second half, but there is the prospect of more scoring. They go for two and fail. They score again, go ahead 15-14, go for two again, and fail again. They score again, kick, and go ahead 22-14. How much more comfortable would they be if they had kicked for two other points? They would have a 10-point lead instead of an eight-point lead.

Obviating the Card by Additional Scoring

To look further into scoring beyond that needed by the team that is behind, let us add scoring to each of the differentials that are on the card. Those differentials are, of course, the ones that tell you to go for two.

First, in each grouping, a net four is added, for you scoring a TD and your opponent a FG; second, a net four is subtracted, for you scoring a FG and your opponent a TD; third, seven is added for the winning team scoring a TD; fourth, three is added for the winning team scoring a FG.

The points you start with, after the scoring, are the result of trying for two and failing. In parentheses are the points you would have if you had tried for one and succeeded.

The word "different" means that the result of a one-pointer would have been different, that it would have either protected you when you were ahead or given you a better chance when you were behind. The word "different" means that the result of kicking would have been different and better.

In 22 of 32 scorings—scorings of more points than those needed by the team that was behind—the result of making a one-pointer would have been different and better. The 10 places where the result would not have been different and better are scattered and would have been difficult to anticipate.

> ***You go for two if you expect only the scoring needed by the team that is left behind.***

+12 +4 = +16 (+17 different)
+12 −4 = +8 (+9 different)
+12 +7 = +19 (+20)
+12 +3 = +15 (+16 different)

+5 +4 = +9 (+10 different)
+5 −4 = +1 (+2)
+5 +7 = +12 (+13)
+5 +3 = +8 (+9 different)

+4 +4 = +8 (+9 different)
+4 −4 = +0 (+1 different)
+4 +7 = +11 (+12 different)
+4 +3 = +7 (+8 different)

+1 +4 = +5 (+6)
+1 −4 = −3 (−2 different)
+1 +7 = +8 (+9 different)
+1 +3 = +4 (+5)

−13 +4 = −9 (−8 different)
−13 −4 = −17 (−16 different)
−13 −7 = −20 (−19)
−13 −3 = −16 (−15 different)

−6 +4 = −2 (−1)
−6 −4 = −10 (−9 different)
−6 −7 = −13 (−12)
−6 −3 = −9 (−8 different)

−5 +4 = −1 (−0 different)
−5 −4 = −9 (−8 different)
−5 −7 = −12 (−11 different)
−5 −3 = −8 (−7 different)

−2 +4 = +2 (+3 different)
−2 −4 = −6 (−5)
−2 −7 = −9 (−8 different)
−2 −3 = −5 (−4)

Heeding Some Advice

You must be careful about going for two too early. The card is not to be followed blindly. You want to have a logical, arithmetic explanation for whatever you do, especially if you lose.

Case: In the 2003 Super Bowl the Oakland Raiders, playing from behind, go for two three times and fail three times. Later, they find themselves down by 13. If they had kicked three times, they would have been down by 10.

Case: Penn State scores to get within 9 of Iowa. A −9 is not on the card, but they have a trick play off of their extra-point formation, a play that will not work unless it is a surprise. The play works, and they get within seven, with 03:59 on the clock. Penn State had had a rough day, and Coach Joe Paterno did not want to have to score 8 and still go through an extra period so he just decided to disregard the card and gamble.

For more cases see Appendix G.

You use the card when the clock tells you that the losing team has time only to catch up.

17

Taking a Safety

The decision that you face involves three considerations: (1) the position of the ball; (2) the weighing of the sure minus two against a probable minus three to a field goal; (3) the time that you will have or that he will not have to score. (1) Most teams count on 13 yards of depth for the punter. (2) The minus two is not always consequential; the minus three is. (3) For scoring needed, you want to have time, but you do not want him to have time.

The position, in which you get the ball back, after each way of turning it over, is not consequential. Neither is the consumption of clock time, since each way should put the ball into play six times before you get it back.

Recognizing the Risk in Punting

The biggest reason for favoring a safety over a punt is that you fear punting. Imagine:

- ball, on the one-inch line,
- last punt, blocked,
- punter, injured,
- new punter, zero game experience,

- wind, against you,
- punt returner, leading the conference,
- field-goal kicker, eight for 10,
- score, ahead by four,
- time, two minutes left.

> ***It is difficult to base a decision on three or more variables, when the variables interrelate.***

That scenario makes you want the relief of a safety. In contrast, imagine:

- ball, on the three-yard line,
- punt protection, good,
- punt coverage, good,
- field-goal kicker, average,
- wind, with you,
- score, ahead by four,
- time, two minutes left.

That scenario leaves you comfortable with a punt. The two examples are at opposite ends of a spectrum of possibilities. Whatever the risk in punting is at decision time, you posit it and let it influence your consideration of other factors.

Case: West Virginia 21, Virginia Tech 16, fourth quarter. UWV gets the ball on its own one-foot line, with 03:51. With 4th-and-eight at 02:33, they take a safety to bring VT to within a FG of a tie. Wise? A punt followed by a VT FG would have brought VT within a FG of a win. UWV has already had a punt blocked, and now they have less than the 13 yards of depth that a punter needs. Wise? UWV wins 21-18.

Approximating Ball Positions

Ball-position possibilities, after a safety and after a punt, do not directly compare:

- After a safety, you can free-kick to about your opponent's 35. You can punt from close to your goalline to about your 35. That difference is about 30 yards.

- If his FG line is the 25 and if he can average five yards per play, he is about four times farther away from that line on his 35 than he is on your 35. For a TD, he would be about twice as far away from his 35 as he would be from yours.
- If you could hold him to three downs after a free kick and after a punt, you would get the ball at about the same position after both, on your 20. His punt, after your free kick, would be from about his 40; his kickoff, after his FG, would be from his 35.

Deciding at Differentials of +6 and –4

You take a safety late in a game when you are backed up to your goal line and the point differential is +6. Going from +6 to +4 is saying that your opponent must still score a TD and that you might as well give him two non-consequential points and then, after your free kick, make him go a long ways for that TD. You do not want to punt and risk having a FG kicked against you and the +6 going to +3.

Plus 6 is the basic differential at which you take a safety. You can also take one, late and backed up, when the differential is -4 and there is time for you to get the ball back and score.

Considering going from -4 to -6 is weighing

- giving your opponent two points, turning the ball over with a free kick, stopping him, taking his punt, and driving for a score to win, against

> *You do not just take a safety. You take it, or you punt.*
> *You give up two points, or you probably give up three.*

- turning it over with a punt, probably yielding a field goal to go down by -7, taking his kickoff, driving for a score to tie, and going into an extra period and outscoring him.

> *There are no other two numbers that have the relationship*
> *to scoring that 6 and 4 have between 7 and 3.*

Going from -4 to -6 is saying that you have to get a TD and you have to stop him, so you might as well be doing it to win, after leaving yourself at -6, rather than possibly to tie, after punting and yielding a FG and leaving yourself at -7.

After both a safety and a punt, if your opponent is stopped after three plays and forced to kick—a punt after your safety kick and a FG after your punt—the time consumed and the ball-position, upon getting the ball back, would be about the same. The ball is put into play six times and time-outs are used, either way.

Before the advent of the two-point play, you could take a safety at +13 and not change the need of two TDs by him. He could not get to +11 without the second TD. You could also do it at -11 and not change the need of two TDs by you. Today, safeties at these differentials are worth keeping in mind for situations where you want to bet that two-pointers—the opponent's if it is +13 and yours if it is -11—will not be made.

In short, you take safeties at +6 and, as long as you will have time to drive for a TD, at -4. For examples of the results of additional scoring see Appendix H.

> ***Plus 6 remains the basic differential at which you take a safety.***

Taking a Safety at Other Differentials

You consider taking a safety in place of punting. You can always punt. In considering, you would take into account

- the risk involved in punting,
- the opponent's point possibilities after your safety and after your punt,
- your points needed after a safety,
- the ball-position possibilities,
- time needed to get the points needed,
- time available,
- the interplay of certain numbers in scoring,
- the percentage chances of things getting done, and
- your gut feeling.

His point possibilities, time needed, the interplay of the numbers, and percentage chances can be fixed beforehand; punting risk, your pending points needed, and time available come from anywhere on spectrums of possibilities; ball-position possibilities are indeterminate; gut feeling is from the moment.

To consider a safety is difficult. Factors interrelate. Risk in punting qualifies everything. Giving up two points and free-kicking from your 20 is difficult to compare with punting from close to your goal line and probably giving up three points. Nothing can be graphed.

Anticipating Your Opponent's Point Possibilities

Before you decide on a safety or a punt, you must guess what the ensuing scoring might be. Before you would get the ball back, you could be down

- by a safety: -2, -5, or -9.
- by a punt: zero, -3, or -7.

As either/or possibilities, the safety/punt possibilities are, realistically,

- -2 or zero, -2 or -3, -5 or -3, -5 or -7, and -9 or -7.

To keep the opponent from getting 3, you probably have to give him 2. The minus two or minus three either/or is the primary one. It should be easier to keep him from getting

- 5 than 3, 7 than 5, and 9 than 7.

For example, if the time remaining is 00:28 at decision-time and if he has one time-out, the zero, the -5, the -7 and the -9 are unlikely. The pair of -2/ -3 is likely.

Whatever way you compare possibilities, you see if one in the pair dominates and, if it does not, you look beyond. For example, if the differential is +7 and it would surely go to +5 or +4, with a -2 or a -3, neither result would dominate. This frees you to consider

- how concerned you are about a blocked punt, and
- how concerned you are about the possible net -5.

In these considerations it is as though you bet. You give your opponent 2 points because you bet that he is going to get 3 if you do not. You yield to him 3 because you bet that he will get 5 if you do not. You risk him getting 5 because you bet that he will get 7 if you do not. You risk giving him 7 because you bet that he will net 9 if you do not. Of course, the more the time remaining, the less the point predictability.

> ***You do not just give up two points.***
> ***You give up two or, probably, you give up three.***

In short, you examine what you think the risk in punting is, and you let that risk qualify all other considerations. Then, you predict what the opponent might do with the ball once it is turned over to him. Then, you consider time, time-outs, and the differential. Then you choose: safety or punt. For examples of the point subtractions which leave +6 and +4 or -4 and -6 see Appendix I.

Allowing for the Interplay of Certain Numbers

The differentials where -2 and -3 get equivalent results are the ones that leave the pairs of

- 2 and 1, 5 and 4, 6 and 5, and 13 and 12.

Those differentials are,

- from the plus side, +4, +7, +8, and +15, and
- from the minus side, -2 , -3, and -10.

You would not go from being ahead to being behind, so a +1 is not included. With the results of -2 and -3 being equatable, would you rather be trying to take the ball away from your opponent in his territory after your free kick, or would you rather have the ball in yours after your punt and his FG?

Again, this is about the choice between (a) giving up 2 and not letting him get 3 more, and (b) giving up 3 but having the ball. For a comparison of resulting needs from -2 and -3 see Appendix K.

Points Needed After Safeties

Taking 32 differentials, from -15 to +16, and subtracting 2 from each leaves you with no two scoring needs that are alike. For example, to go from +9 to +7 is to go from your opponent needing a TD and a FG to beat you to his needing a TD to tie you, and there is no other change like this in 32 possibilities. For all 32 see Appendix J.

Estimating the Time Needed to Get the Points Needed after a Safety

This is about minimum times for scoring, for you if you are behind and for your opponent if you are ahead. Rough estimations must suffice.

When you are behind and must get the ball back after your free kick, you will use your time-outs when he is on offense and, you must hope, he will execute just three plays and punt. When you are ahead and must stop him after your free kick, he will use his time-outs on offense and, you must hope, he will not have enough time to score.

The numbers showing the times to the scores are made up of 5s, 10s, 15s, 35s, and 40s.

- If you are behind, you do not want to run out of seconds before you thought you would, so you estimate high for consumption —10 for a play, a punt, or a FG, and 15 for the ref.
- If you are ahead, you do not want your opponent to have seconds when you thought he would not, so you estimate low—5 for a play, a punt, or a FG, and 10 for the ref.
- Plays for which there are time-outs—10 for yours and 5 for his.
- The safety and the free kick are always 5 each. An onside kick is zero.
- The average between snaps for the team that is behind is 15. The average for the team that is ahead is 35.

An estimated gain per play on the way to a FG kicked from the 25 is 10 yards. An estimated gain between the FG line and the goal line is five yards.

Plays on the way to your FG after the safety kick and your opponent's punt are six; on the way to your TD, eleven. Plays on the way to his FG after the safety kick are four; to his TD, nine. Plays on the way to your FG after recovering your onside kick are three; to your TD, eight.

Minimums for *You* to Score Once after a Safety				
Your Time-Outs	3	2	1	0
FG	02:20	02:50	03:20	03:50
TD	03:35	04:05	04:35	05:05
Minimums For *You* To Score Twice				
FG and TD	04:20	04:50	05:20	05:50
Two TDs	05:35	06:05	06:35	07:05
Minimums For *Him* To Score Once				
His Time-Outs	3	2	1	0
FG	00:40	00:50	01:00	01:10
TD	01:55	02:05	02:15	02:25

As rough as these numbers are, if they are to be used, they need to be on carefully prepared cards.

The 03:20 for the minimum for you to score one FG is built this way:

> 10 taking the safety; 35 and 35 for his two plays; 10 for a play with a time-out; 10 for a punt; 5 getting you started; 90 for a six-play FG drive at 15 seconds per play; 5 for the kick; total 03:20.

The 06:35 for the minimum for you to score two TDs is built this way:

> 10 taking the safety; 35 and 35 for two plays; 10 for his play and your time-out; 10 for his punt; 5 getting you started; 165 for your 11-play TD drive; 0 for the onside kick; 5 getting you started; 120 for your eight-play TD drive; total 06:35.

The numbers above say that, if there is anything less as you consider a safety, there will not be normal time for the team that is behind to get the points it needs. You want to have more than the times shown for you. You want your opponent to have less than the times shown for him.

> ***What is required to make up for the yielding of two points and possession of the ball is different for every point differential from −15 to +16.***

You do not take a safety if you are behind and out of time-outs and your opponent can execute three plays and consume the remaining time. You go for the first down.

You do take a safety if you can sacrifice the points and he will not have time to return your free kick and drive against you.

> **Case:** Going for another national championship, Georgia Southern is ahead of Montana 27-23, with 01:15 and the ball on their 15. Montana has two time-outs, so GSU cannot consume the remaining time without making a first down. GSU's QB sneaks. Time-out. GSU's QB sweeps. Time-out. Now 01:05. GSU's QB sweeps. On the 4th-down GSU lets the 25-second counter run down and takes a five-yard penalty. Tension! Complexity! In the booth they are wondering if Tiger Woods played golf at Yale in the early 1900s. Should GSU punt or should they take a safety? A punt might get blocked or returned for a winning TD. A safety would leave GSU ahead by two and vulnerable to a FG. GSU takes a safety, with its punter. Montana cannot answer. GSU is the national champion.

Estimating Percentage Chances in Getting Things Done

About percentage chances, remember that different coaches estimate them differently and that they change with fatigue, injuries, and weather. Following are one coach's estimates:

10%	getting a punt blocked
80%	getting a FG kicked against you if you punt
40%	getting a TD scored against you if you punt
40%	getting a FG kicked against you if you take a safety
20%	getting a TD scored against you if you take a safety
99%	kicking an extra point
33%	making a two-pointer
10%	recovering an onside kick
50%	winning in an extra period
60%	preventing more than a normal return of any kick

The chance of getting a punt blocked varies with the location of the ball. It varies, probably, from 20% to 10%.

Before having to make decisions, you want to have thought through your positions on everything but especially on

- playing for a tie, going for two, and kicking onside.

In addition to these percentage chances, you must consider your own and your opponent's offense, defense, kick protections and returns, clock management and present state of mind.

An assumption in this material is that the team that is playing from behind will want to kick an extra point to tie the score and have a 50 percent chance of winning in overtime rather than to try a two-pointer and have a 33 percent chance of winning outright. In a third extra period, by the college rules, a try for two is imposed.

Considering the Most Likely Scenarios

If the risk in punting is nominal and if you want to anticipate only the possibilities of (a) taking a safety and giving the opponent 2 but no more and (b) punting and yielding 3 but no more, this is how you might decide from the differentials:

-1   Safety. Do not risk going beyond −3.
-2   Either. Either -4 or -5 will leave you needing a TD.
-3   Either. Either -5 or -6 will leave you needing a TD.
-4   Safety. Do not risk going to -7.
-5   Punt. You can give up -3 but not -5. Also, if you can hold the opponent to a field goal, -8 with the ball is better than -7 without it.
-6   Safety. Do not risk going beyond -8.
-7   Safety. Do not risk going beyond -9.
-8   Safety. Do not risk going beyond -10.
-9   Safety. Do not risk going beyond -11.
-10 Either. Either -12 or -13 will leave you needing two TDs.
-11 Safety. At -13 you can win with two TDs.
-12 Safety. Do not risk going beyond -14.
-13 Safety. Do not risk going beyond -15.

0   Punt. Do not automatically put yourself behind.
+1   Punt. Same reason.
+2   Either. If the punting situation is dire and time is short and if you would not mind taking a 50-50 chance in overtime, take a safety.
+3   Safety. Would it be harder to yield a field goal and have to win in an extra period or to keep your opponent from getting a net +5? The former.
+4   Either. Either +2 or +1 will leave him needing a FG.
+5   Punt. +2 with the ball is better than +3 without it.
+6   Safety.
+7   Either. Either +5 or +4 will leave him needing a TD.
+8   Punt. You can risk giving the opponent 7 but not 9.
+9   Punt. Do not risk giving him 9.
+10 Safety. Nine would leave him behind.

Honoring Your Gut Feeling

From your gut alone can you get decisions like the following?

- "They almost blocked our last punt. They'll be crazy to block the next one. Take a safety."

- "If we take a safety, they'll get seven more and have nine, sure as anything. Punt it!"
- "Ahead three to zero. Thirty seconds left. Their return man is ranked nationally. Take a safety." And Air Force beats Washington 3-2 in 1963. It was my call.

Choosing Who Takes the Safety

The possibilities are the QB, with dropback pass protection, and the punter. The problem is to get to the end zone without getting tackled, to keep the ball alive, and to get across a boundary line without getting tackled and risking a fumble.

The considerations that favor the QB are

- the dropback-pass blocking assignments that specialize in getting bodies on bodies and that identify a rusher who cannot be blocked,
- the chance he has to escape around an outside-in block by an offset RB and to run to the sideline,
- the center being a blocker,
- his experience in handling and carrying the ball, and
- keeping pass defenders out of the rush.

The considerations that favor the punter are

- depth, and
- disguising intent.

Figure 17-1 shows the blocking for a scramble pass with (a) the QB setting up short to help the RB with his outside-in block, (b) the line blockers losing the rushers to their right, and (c) the QB giving ground and escaping around the RB's block.

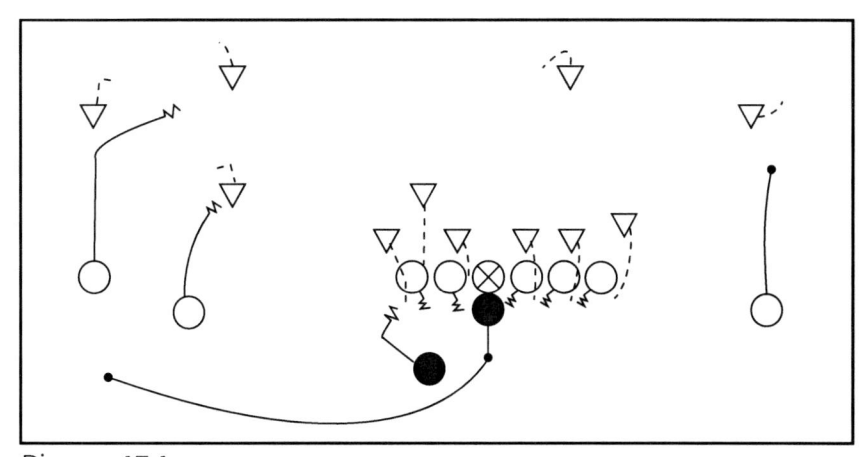

Diagram 17-1

18

Keeping the Clock Moving

Avoiding a Huge Mistake

Here is a situation:

> The game is ending. You are ahead by four. You have the ball on your own 15, 2nd down, with 01:40, 01:39 on a moving clock. Your opponent has no time-outs remaining.

Here is what you had better not do:

- Go for a first down that you do not need, hand the ball off unnecessarily, fumble, and lose.
- Start taking a knee, end up having to punt, get the punt blocked, and lose.
- Lose and not be able to explain why you did what you did.

Case: Tennessee, leading 19-9 in the fourth quarter, sees Southern Mississippi make it 19-16 at 00:55. USM has two time-outs. Tennessee gets USM's onside kick. The clock shows 00:52. Do they need a first down? This material says, no, assuming that they will be executing time-consuming plays. Tennessee runs into the line twice—these are not time-consuming plays—and USM calls time-out twice. With 00:43 showing, Tennessee takes a knee. This is clearly a mistake. As a result they have to punt. They had better do it securely. They do and win.

Case: Alabama is ahead of Vanderbilt and has a first down, with 01:13 on a stopped clock. Vandy has one time-out. The Alabama QB can simply keep the ball alive and consume the time, but he hands it off. Vandy uses its time-out. Two more handoffs, at 01:08 and 00:20, end the game. But you should not hand the ball off if you do not have to. Ask the NFL play-caller who, some years ago, called for a handoff, lost a fumble and a game, caused an uproar in the media, and got fired two days later.

Measuring Time Consumption

Using low numbers for execution time and ref time—you do not want to be surprised to find yourself with time you thought you were going to be rid of. Consumption times in seconds are

- for falling on the ball—2,
- for keeping the ball alive—5,
- for a play for which your opponent has a time-out—2 or 5, depending on whether you will be falling on the ball or keeping it alive,
- for the Ref—10
- for the 25-second counter—20,
- for the time before and including a 1st-down play—25,
- for a segment of time between the endings of two plays—35, and
- for this segment when you fall on the ball—32.

Four "alive" plays, if the clock cannot be stopped, can consume 130 seconds, or 02:10. Add it up:

```
 25   before and by the 1st-down play, if no change of possession
 35   before and by the 2nd-down play
 35   before and by the 3rd-down play
 35   before and by the 4th-down play
─────
130   or two minutes and 10 seconds
```

The clock always stops, at least temporarily, after a 4th-down play.

Four "kneel-down" plays, if the clock is stopped until the snap before a 1st-down play and stopped by time-outs after the 1st-, 2nd-, and 3rd-down plays and temporarily after the 4th-down play, can consume as little as 8 seconds. Add it up:

    2   by the 1st-down play, out of a stopped clock
    2   by the 2nd-down play
    2   by the 3rd-down play
    2   by the 4th-down play

    8

Comparing 130 to 8—that is dramatic!

Falling on the ball is generally better than taking a knee. It allows the QB to wait a little longer before he must avoid getting smothered. Also, with RBs folding over him, it can cause the ref to take a little longer getting the ball ready.

Counting Time Consumption on Your Fingers

The best way to keep from making a huge mistake is to have a clock-management specialist

- hold up four fingers in front of his face,
- let each represent the time up to and including one of the four downs in a series,
- close a finger for each down that is gone,,
- apply 2s, 5s, 25s, 32s, and 35s to plays not yet run,
- add up, on the upright fingers, what you can consume,
- compare the sum with the clock and, if there is more on the upright fingers than there is on the clock, expect that the time will be consumed.

> *A clock-management specialist can do things that a head coach or a play-caller cannot do.*

In the opening example, the time on the moving clock was 01:40, 01:39 at the end of the 1st-down play. With this, do you need a first down? Close the first finger because the 1st-down play is over. Add up three 35s—105 or 01:45. So you do not need a first down to keep your opponent from getting the ball. Can you fall on the ball? Add up three 32s—96, which is 01:36. No, you cannot just fall on the ball. You must keep the ball alive to consume 01:39. Taking a knee too soon results in many losses each year.

Case: Pittsburgh, ahead of West Virginia 23-17 in the fourth quarter, gets a first down on the UWV four, with 01:36. UWV has two time-outs. Can Pitt take a knee?

The booth says they can. Let us see. Before the ball will be snapped, at least 20 seconds will be gone. Taking a knee will take two seconds. UWV will call time-out, and 01:14 will remain. Taking a knee out of a stopped clock will take two. UWV will call time-out, and 01:12 will remain. Taking a knee again and not stopping the clock will leave about 40 seconds for the 4th down. Taking a knee would be a serious mistake. Pitt must actually score to keep UWV from having a chance to win.

Exercising Your Fingers

Imagine: 00:54 on a stopped clock, 2nd down, opponent with one time-out. **Count:** Close one finger, because the 1st down is gone. Add 5 for the 2nd-down play, 5 for the time-out play, and 35 for the 4th play. You get 45 seconds, so you need a first down.

Imagine: 01:51 on a temporarily-stopped clock, 1st down, opponent with no time-outs. **Count:** Open all four fingers. Add, for the four downs, 25, 35, 35, and 35. You get 130 seconds or 02:10. Subtract 12 seconds, for falling on the ball rather than keeping it alive, to see if you can fall on the ball. Yes, you can.

Separating the Procedural from the Decisional

All of this is procedural. When it gets decisional is when you are ahead and it is 3rd-and-five on your 40 with 00:51 showing on a stopped clock and your opponent has no time-outs; when you can run and consume 35 seconds but, if you fail to make a first down, you will have to punt and play defense for two or three plays; when, if you pass and succeed, the game is over but, if you fail, he will have more than 40 seconds. Dilemmas make it decisional.

Being Thorough

Do you ever play slow just because you are ahead? No, not perceptibly. Intensity levels are difficult enough to maintain without slowing the pace. Besides, any time a coach wants to use up most of the counter, he can do it imperceptibly by calling for motions and shifts and by substituting laboriously, while having the QB ensure that there is no delay penalty. This is what is referred to as DELIBERATE play.

Going out-of-bounds can add a half dozen plays to your opponent's offense. Getting too close and getting knocked out-of-bounds can do the same.

Case: With a Heisman Trophy and a national championship on the line, Oklahoma has the ball on its own 18, ahead of Kansas State 24-17, with 04:04. They want a

> ***You do not want to hand the ball off and risk a fumble, when you did not need to hand it off.***

time-consuming drive. The ball should stay inbounds, but twice on their drive it goes out. Why? Because ballcarriers got too close to the boundary and got knocked out. OU gets a FG but leaves KSU 01:19. If the ballcarriers had stayed inbounds, KSU might have had 00:19.

Figure 18-1 shows cup protection for keeping the QB alive for five seconds or more. Two TEs are essential. Big backs are valuable. The offset back is there, first, to recover a fumbled snap and, second, to be a personal protector.

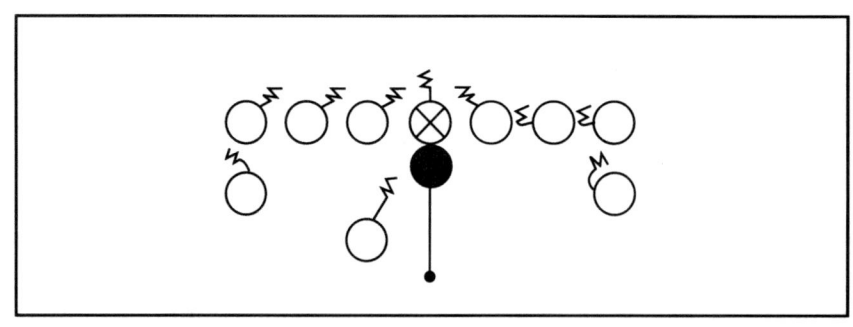

Diagram 18-1

An inbounds QB Sweep is shown in Figure 18-2, with a two-TE personnel unit and a TE-over formation. It should keep the clock moving for more than five seconds. The unbalanced line is to minimize the chance of facing penetration off the playside edge.

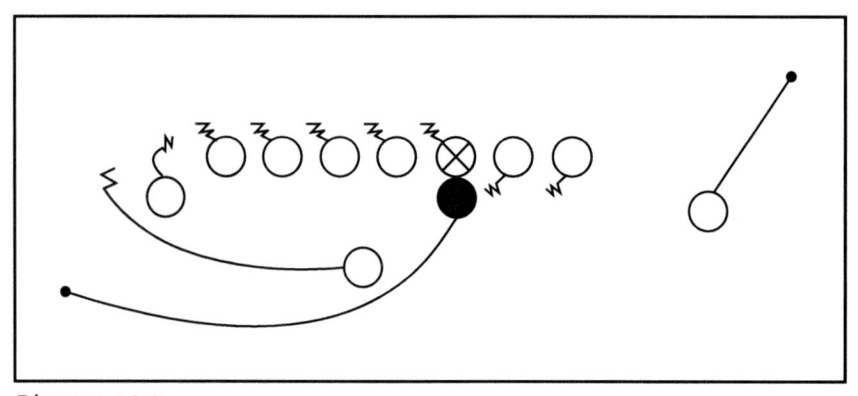

Diagram 18-2

When you want to consume maximum time on a play, are you better off with the QB fighting to stay on his feet behind cup protection or with him running a sweep? Both are good.

Deep in the opponent's territory, you do not have the same problem that you have in your own territory, where your 4th-down play may have to be a dreaded punt. You do not have to consider passing on 3rd down to get a first down. You can run on 3rd and 4th downs and, if you fail to make a first down, you will leave your opponent with poor field position. The decision on when to fall on the ball is, of course, the same in both territories.

Case: Michigan State, ahead of Marshall by 10, drives to Marshall's six and has a 2nd down, with 00:49. Marshall is out of time-outs. MSU runs and scores. Should they have taken a knee? Games are lost every year by teams that go for points they do not need.

A defender who gets a turnover should get to the ground if all his QB is going to have to do is keep the ball alive or fall on it.

What if you do not need to score to win? You do not try to score.

Incidentally, it makes no more sense to refer to move-the-clock offense as four-minute offense than it does to refer to stop-the-clock offense as two-minute offense.

For additional cases see Appendix L.

You do not want to have a punt blocked when you did not need to punt and, then, have to explain why you punted.

Using Printed Numbers for Decision-Making

Table 18-1 shows the times, at the end of a game, when you

- may fall on the ball,
- must keep the ball alive, or
- must make a first down.

The times are made up of these numbers:

:02 for falling on the ball,
:05 for keeping the ball alive,

:10 for the ref getting the ball ready,

:20 for bleeding the 25-second counter,

35 for executing a play with the clock moving

The estimates are low, as they must always be when you want time to expire. For the play-caller, the table does not take the place of counting on four fingers, although a clock-management specialist could follow it and advise from it.

At the top left of Table 18-1, under the 3 for opponent's time-outs, the "1st, Stopped" and the ":08 or less" mean that

- it is 1st down,
- the clock is stopped until the snap,
- the opponent can stop the clock with time-outs, after the 1st, 2nd, and 3rd downs,
- :02 will be consumed for each time the QB falls on the ball,
- the clock will stop temporarily after the 4th-down play, and
- the QB can fall on the ball.

At the bottom right of Table 18-1 under the zero for opponent's time-outs, the "4th, Moving" and the ":36 or more" mean that

- it is the 4th down,
- the clock will not stop,
- the ref will take 10 seconds and the QB can bleed 20 out of the 25-second counter, so 35 seconds can be consumed, and
- if :36 or more shows, the calling of a play that has a chance to get a first down is in order.

Using the table, a clock-management specialist could, on a 2nd-down play with the clock moving and with the opponent having zero time-outs,

- see 01:35, 01:34 on the clock,
- have a finger on the right box of numbers,
- see that 01:35 is between 01:31 and 01:45 for keeping the ball alive, and
- advise "alive".

The play-caller could have, on the tip of his tongue, his play for getting a first down and could, upon hearing "alive", change quickly and call the "alive" play of his choice.

Consuming the Final Seconds

Down, Decision	Opponent's Time-Outs			
	3	2	1	0
1st, Stopped				
Fall	:08 or less	:36 or less	1:04 or less	1:32 or less
Alive	:09 to :20	:37 to :50	1:05 to 1:20	1:33 to 1:50
First down	:21 or more	:51 or more	1:21 or more	1:51 or more
1st, Stopped Temporarily				
Fall	:28 or less	:56 or less	1:24 or less	1:52 or less
Alive	:29 to :40	:57 to 1:10	1:25 to 1:40	1:53 to 2:10
First down	:41 or more	1:11 or more	1:41 or more	2:11 or more
2nd, stopped				
Fall	X	:06 or less	:34 or less	1:02 or less
Alive	X	:07 to :15	:35 to :45	1:03 to 1:15
First down	X	:16 or more	:46 or more	1:16 or more
2nd, Moving				
Fall	X	:34 or less	1:02 or less	1:30 or less
Alive	X	:35 to :45	1:03 to 1:15	1:31 to 1:45
First down	X	:46 or more	1:16 or more	1:46 or more
3rd, Stopped				
Fall	X	X	:04 or less	:32 or less
Alive	X	X	:05 to :10	:33 to :40
First down	X	X	:11 or more	:41 or more
3rd, Moving				
Fall	X	X	:32 or less	1:00 or less
Alive	X	X	:33 to :40	1:01 to 1:10
First down	X	X	:41 or more	1:11 or more
4th, Stopped				
Fall	X	X	X	:02 or less
Alive	X	X	X	:03 to :05
First down	X	X	X	:06 or more
4th, Moving				
Fall	X	X	X	:32 or less
Alive	X	X	X	:33 to :35
First down	X	X	X	:36 or more

Table 18-1

19

Preparing the Quarterback

A clock-management team comprises the decision-making head coach, a play-caller in the pressbox, his distance-to-go observer, a clock-management specialist beside the head coach with numbers on cards, and the quarterback.

In a game that is controlled almost entirely by coaches, stop-the-clock offense can force control onto the QB. After coaches have made a decision on the sideline, the QB is the arbiter on the field.

Case: The Carolina Panthers need a TD to beat the Green Bay Packers. With 00:54, Carolina completes a pass on the Green Bay five. It is 4th-and goal. The Carolina QB looks idle. The booth is urgent about getting the remaining time-out called, but the QB is in control and has one of those situations where bleeding is absolutely required before calling a time-out.

This chapter is meant to be a guide and a checklist for preparing the quarterback.

Managing Time by the QB, on the Field

The quarterback is the one who

- calls the quickest time-out,
- hears the ref's whistle to declare the ball ready for play,

- asks when a stopped clock will start,
- watches the 25-second and 40-second counters,
※ • controls the speed of play, and
- sees before a snap if the time remaining is enough for the play called.

He must know how to consume time, with 10 other players not knowing they are doing it—DELIBERATE play, it is called here. He can call for the snap with 00:05 left on the counter and, before that, he can take longer giving instructions in the huddle and at the line, all the while making the rhythm seem normal. There is plenty that he can do if he knows how to coordinate the pace of play with the time on the counter.

He must know how to speed things up by hustling and encouraging hustle, without losing the feeling of normal play—HUSTLE play, it is called here.

He must know how to play FAST and SLOW but, when he does, all players must know what is going on.

> **The clock will inescapably involve the QB in the most pressurized and difficult of managing problems.**

Case: LSU is coming off of its own nine in the second quarter, behind South Carolina 3-14, with 04:56. Consuming the time, they make first downs at 04:07, 03:06, and 01:59. They cross midfield with 00:14, hit a pass for a first down at 00:01, call time-out, and make a kick. The QB kept the clock moving when he wanted to, stopped it when he wanted to, called time-out when he wanted to, and scored when he wanted to.

He must know how to keep playing FAST when he is unsure about

- the ball being out-of-bounds beyond the first-down line,
- what the clock is doing,
- what the officials are talking about,
- a measurement being called for, or
- the head coach hurrying on the FG personnel.

He should know how to help when the play-caller does not have his usual 15 seconds between the time he knows the down-and-distance and the time the wasting of seconds begins; i.e., know how to help when there is an injury, a measurement, a penalty, or game administration. On a measurement or a penalty, he must know (a) how to have his team lined up and a play ready to go if there is no first down or penalty yardage, and (b) how to take a signal for another play, in case the chains or the ball is moved, and he must know how to get the ball snapped at the toot of the whistle.

When a time-out is to be called the instant the ballcarrier goes down, the QB must know how to position himself in front of the white cap while watching the ballcarrier and how to both call and signal instantly.

Case: Cincinnati is ahead of Ohio State, just before the half. They have 1st-and-10 on the 50, with 00:26 and one time-out. The QB scrambles for eight yards. The time-out is called at 00:12, after a major waste of time. They pass and pass again and, luckily, have 00:01 left for their 4th down. With a once in a lifetime chance against Ohio State, they do not want to come that close to losing a down to the clock.

If the ref is going to consume the final seconds preparing to signal that the ball is ready, there is nothing the QB can do short of calling a time-out. The ball remains dead and a whistle is to prevent the possible consumption of playing time.

Leading, on the Field

The quarterback must know how to be a coach on the field, with instructions like the following:

- "If you don't have a first down, get out-of-bounds. If you have a first down, stay inbounds and fight for yardage."
- "We're in slow play. Bust your asses to stay with your blocks. That'll create piles."
- "Give me tight cup protection, and I'll see how long I can keep the ball alive."
- "Don't zig and zag and let that time expire. I'll call the time-out as you go down."

Case: Miami goes ahead of Florida State in the fourth quarter 24-20 and leaves 00:42. FSU gets to Miami's 32 in five plays and has a first down and a time-out but only 00:10. They try to substitute. The clock starts. Time-out is called at 00:05. The kick misses. It was from too far away. The way to squeeze in another play in this situation is to (a) have a formation that does not need to be changed, (b) beat the chain crew and the ref and get a snap at 00:09, (c) have an off-tackle play aimed at the goalposts and have a back who understands that he is not to zig and zag and consume all of the time and (d) have the QB in the white cap's face calling time-out if the ballcarrier goes down.

Executing Certain Plays

The quarterback must know how to ensure that a pass will be either past a line—first-down line or goal line—or incomplete. Even if receivers make mistakes, he must ensure.

He must know how to ensure that one particular and well-practiced pass will not result in a sack or an interception. On that pass he must know how to instruct the blockers that, for his promise of a well-timed release, there is to be no chance of a holding penalty.

> ***Rules have been written and rewritten to keep coaches and players from beating them.***

Changing Plays

The quarterback's most pressurized job is at the LOS, where he must ensure that there is time to execute the play that has been called. To make sure, he must know the time barriers beyond which the plays must not go. Example:

If he sees that there is not time for a spike after a first down, he must get the ball into the end zone with a pass. Ideally, he will have the pass already called and will spike only if he sees 00:03 or more.

To learn his job, he must work beside the play-caller in the indoor simulation, watch the little stopwatches, and be ready to change from

- a regular play to a first-down pass,
- a first-down pass to a boundary pass,
- a boundary pass to an end-zone pass, or
- a spike to an end-zone pass.

Case: In a Rose Bowl game, a Washington State spike took the clock down to 00:00. The QB, upon seeing that he had 00:02 on a first down clock, should have signaled for an end-zone pass.

Bleeding the Clock

If bleeding is going to take an unusually long time, the QB must know how to talk to the team, as he would if he were checking off, so the snap will seem to be in the normal rhythm.

When bleeding down to time for a final play—00:06 for a spike, 00:04 for a time-out, 00:04 for the initiating of a play or kick—he wants to watch whichever clock shows fewer seconds. Through the game he has been watching the 25-second counter. Now his concern is the end of the game. He does not want to be watching the 25-second counter, with the scoreboard clock showing fewer seconds, and bleed the game away. Likewise, he does not want to be watching the scoreboard clock, with the 25-second counter showing fewer, and get a delay penalty. He wants to practice in simulation with two clocks until there is no possibility of a mistake.

Managing in Wind Near a Change of Quarters

Even when a coach is doing it all—watching the clock, calling for speeds of play, calling plays, and calling time-outs—the QB wants to know the objective. For example, in wind at a change of quarters, the objective is,

- against the wind, to use move-the-clock offense so, if a first down is not made, the quarter will change before the punt or FG kick, and
- with the wind, to use stop-the-clock offense so, if a first down is not made, the quarter will not change before the punt or FG kick.

Holding for a Field-Goal Attempt

On a 4th-down field-goal attempt, if the snap is bobbled and the kick cannot be made, the QB must know how to yell for and execute an emergency running pass with receivers separating themselves in the end zone.

On a 3rd-down field-goal attempt—this would be to have another down in case anything goes wrong—if the snap is bobbled, he must know how to yell for and execute an emergency incomplete pass. The 3rd-down attempt is best suited for overtime, when there is no concern about saving time for the opponent to return a kickoff.

Taking a Safety and Bleeding Time

The best way to take a safety is with the QB. The best way for the QB to take a safety is to get to the end zone by dropback pass protection, which distributes blockers and identifies the defender for whom there is no blocker and whom the QB may have to beat.

The best way to bleed time is to get into the end zone, run to a boundary line, and stay alive until it is time to jump across the line to keep from getting hit. The best way to get to a boundary line is to (a) take a short drop to bait an end-of-line rusher, (b) have an RB hook-block that rusher, then (c) lose ground and sprint around that block.

Managing Noise

In college, as of 2006, there is no rule by which the referee can interrupt the game because of deafening noise. The QB is expected to communicate with hand-signals. Some noise can interfer with the verbal calling of plays in huddles, so hand-signalling is expected to go to linemen as well as to back and ends.

Noise invites the use of shotgun formations, which do not require verbal snap signals.

It is possible to play perfectly good football with only a play-caller in the pressbox using his voice.

> **There would be no bigger mistake than bleeding the 25-second counter and having the scoreboard clock go to 00:00.**

Squeezing in Next-to-the-Last Plays

In squeezing in a next-to-the-last play, the quarterback must be certain that time will not expire before the last play. His concerns are the plays out of first-down or moving clocks. His barriers are the play-caller's conservative barriers:

- 00:45, 00:44 with the clock moving and with a call that can leave it moving,
- 00:35, 00:34 with it moving and with a call that can leave it only stopped or temporarily stopped,
- 00:35 with a first down and with a call that can leave it moving,
- 00:30, 00:29 with it moving and with a call that will leave it stopped,
- 00:20 with a first down and with a call that can leave it only stopped or temporarily stopped,
- 00:15 with a first down and with a call that will leave it stopped.

These are the barriers for penultimate plays, the barriers for protecting final plays. The QB must know them and be able to change plays for which there is not going to be enough time.

> **When a next-to-the-last play is being squeezed in, the QB at the LOS is the final protector of the time needed for the last play.**

Being Thorough

He must know how to

- spike, throwing the ball forward and avoiding linemen's feet,
- get the ball into the end zone on a pass for two points, no matter what,
- take an intentional delay penalty,
- keep from losing seconds when there is an injury, a measurement, a penalty, or game administration,
- fall on the ball, rather than take a knee, to consume an extra second,
- keep the ball alive by running wide but avoiding, absolutely, getting forced out-of-bounds.

Practicing

Rules control coaching. Nothing controls practicing. An older QB can guide younger QBs in simulation, with the table-top field, the stopwatches, the tension, and the works. The guide can learn as much as the guided.

Telling You What He Thinks

In consideration of the investment that a QB must make in clock management, he should be given opportunities and encouragement to say what he thinks. Examples:

- If he does not want to spike away a down and two seconds, he should be able to say so. Saving just the two seconds might give him another play.
- If he wants time-outs to be used to give him more plays, not to relieve pressure, he should be able to say so.
- If he does not want to lose seconds huddling on measurements, penalties, or game administration, he should be able to say so.

- If he wants ballcarriers who have first downs to stay inbounds and get all the yardage they can, rather than going out-of-bounds to stop a clock that was going to stop and stay stopped for 15 seconds, he should be able to say so.
- If he does not want to waste time practicing the first parts of two-minute drills but wants to get right down to repetitions on the hard parts that come in the last 30 seconds, he should be able to say so.

Case: Michigan hits a long second-quarter pass on the Florida eight, with 00:34. They have one time-out. There is a signal from the sideline to spike. The QB does. With 1st-and-goal in a situation where the 4th down will be used for a FG, a great QB is instructed to throw one-third of his chances into the ground. There is no redeeming factor in doing this. It is simply inconsiderate and wrong.

Case: Michigan is losing to Ohio State 9-14 in the fourth quarter. With a first down on their 46, they spike at 00:20 and leave 00:19. With another first down at the OSU 24, they spike at 00:09 and leave 00:07. They throw, incomplete, and have 00:01. They throw again, incomplete. They lose. Spiking was not the reason, but it might have been.

Case: Tennessee is up by two in the second quarter over Florida and has 2nd-and-two on the +24, with 02:02 and all three time-outs. They run for what appears to be a first down. The clock moves. Finally, at 01:35, it is stopped for a measurement. Unwisely, Tennessee huddles. It is 3rd-and-inches. They make it, and the 1st-down play starts at 01:16. In a clock drive, two plays were executed in 46 seconds. Why? Because of the uncertainty about the measurement, the unclear need for a time-out, and the huddling. A few plays later, after a time-out at 00:24, there is a fumble. Players fight for the ball. Finally, at 00:10, the clock is stopped temporarily while the ref sorts out the players. Tennessee has recovered. Unwisely, they huddle. The ball is readied. The clock starts. Time-out is called at 00:05. The kick, despite it all, is good.

20

Practicing

Without constant practice the coaches will be nervous and undecided when mustering for the game; without constant practice, the head coach will be wavering and irresolute when the crisis is at hand.

The sentence above is a paraphrasing from the strategy classic, *"The Art of War"*, written by China's Sun Tzu 2500 years ago and, they say, used by most of the best generals throughout history.

There is no way for you to be ready to manage the clock without constant practice.

Beginning Securely

A controller controls. In simulation, he controls the situations that make practice possible. Advice to him:

Begin with success. Build ability within stability. Never overload. At the point of any overload, talk, then back up.

This stuff is difficult. If practice is allowed to embarrass, it will be avoided. And the ones most vulnerable to embarrassment—the head coach and the QBs—are the ones who can least afford to avoid it.

Getting Started

A simulator has

- a table-top football field, about 2 x 4 1/2 feet,
- two special stopwatches, to represent the game clock and the 25-second counter,
- a strip to represent the chains,
- a pencil to show ball-position,
- two chairs at one end for the head coach and the QB,
- one chair at the other end for the operator of the watches, who can be another QB,
- one chair on one side for the controller, who can double as the clock-management specialist,
- one chair on the other side for the pressbox play-caller.

To force decision-making, the controller wants to know, ahead of time, where the ball is to be and what the clock is to show for the decision and, hence, where the first down needs to be. Since he is in control, he can have

- the offense gain or lose any yardage,
- the ref take more or less time with his process,
- the clock stop or keep moving, and
- measurements, penalties, and player-equipment problems interrupt.

Using the Time-Outs

To get started, do drives for touchdowns from about your own 20, each time with 02:00 and three time-outs. Mix plays and use a time-out every time the clock does not get stopped. Next, do drives for field goals and use time-outs the same way, until you are past the FG line and plan to be running on your penultimate play and want your third time-out for getting FG personnel onto the field for an unhurried kick. Overcome the natural hesitation to use time-outs to add plays.

Feeling What Boundary Plays and First-Down Passes Will Do

Next, do drives for touchdowns, with no time-outs. Use your clock-stopping boundary run and your boundary and first-down passes. Drive until these weapons begin to feel almost as effective as time-outs in stopping the clock.

Driving with One Time-out

Next, drive with one time-out, which can make all penults approximately the same in time consumption.

In going for a FG, it is critical to have the ballcarrier trained to take instructions not to zig and zag and consume time, and to have the QB trained to wait in front of the white cap to call the time-out the instant the ballcarrier goes down.

In simulation try to get to a field-goal line and experience

- not getting there and needing one more play and being confronted with times on both sides of the basic barriers for getting off one clock-stopping penult—times representing both plenty of time and not enough time, with not enough meaning to call a less time-consuming play—the basic barriers being:
  - moving clock—00:30, 00:29
  - first-down clock—00:15, and
  - stopped clock—00:10,
- not getting there, failing to get the clock stopped, and using the time-out without hesitation;
- short of the line, after failing to get the clock stopped and having to use the last time-out, changing strategy to depend on passes, a possible hurry-on, a possible spike, a possible interruption snap or, if the line is not reached, an end-zone pass;
- short of the FG line, with a first down at 00:05, using the time-out, because there is time for only one play whether a spike is used or not;
- using it anywhere after a clock-stopping play leaves 00:04 or less, using it just to have extra time to advise the players on the kick or the final play;
- getting there and into the zone where you do not want to risk holding/sack/interception, failing to get the clock stopped, and saving the time-out for later use to get FG personnel onto the field because you will save as many seconds by using it then as you would save by using it now;
- getting there with 4th-and-four and 00:22, 00:21, bleeding down to 00:04, and calling time-out.
- getting there with a 1st-down play, seeing 00:31, 00:30, not wanting to pass, wanting to get closer, being protected by the time-out, trying a boundary run and (a) getting the clock stopped and a second run executed, and (b) not getting the clock stopped and using the time-out;
- getting there with 1st-and-goal on the eight, seeing 02:22, playing SLOW with the first three snaps at approximately

- □ 01:59,
- □ 01:14, and
- □ 00:30,

 calling time-out at 00:04, kicking on 4th down, leaving him 00:00, and winning;
- getting there with a first down on the +30 at 00:29, wanting to get closer but not wanting to risk losing yardage or the ball, having to decide between (a) a run, a bleed, the time-out, and a kick and (b) the risk of two passes to gain 10 yards and maybe more, the time-out if necessary, and possibly a much easier kick;
- being there on 2nd down, not wanting to pass, seeing 00:23, 00:22, not being able to safely squeeze in even a boundary run, and having to let 20 seconds tick off before calling the time-out;
- same situation but being willing to pass, using the time-out first, calling a boundary pass and a first-down-pass/spike package, and kicking.

This script and one more are to serve as examples. All of the needed scripts are not included. A controller must practice creating situations just as a play-caller must practice choosing plays.

Driving without a Time-Out

Before beginning, review that

- the game must end with the ball in the end zone;
- a hurry-on is for 4th-down;
- a hurry-on or a spike requires the same time that any penult requires;
- if the clock is moving, a running penult needs 00:45, 00:44, a first-down-pass penult, 00:35, 00:34, and a boundary-pass penult, 00:30, 00:29,
- if the clock is temporarily stopped, the three are 00:35, 00:20, and 00:15,
- if stopped, 00:30, 00:15, and 00:10,
- the field-goal line is always exactly established, so an instant decision can be based on it.

Try to get to the established field-goal line and experience

- not getting there with a 3rd-down play, seeing 00:21, 00:20, and having to throw for the end zone;
- not getting there and facing a 3rd-and-short, seeing 00:36, 00:35, not having time to run and fail, having time only for a first-down pass;

- same situation, seeing 00:31, 00:30, and having time only for a boundary pass;
- not getting a first down, seeing 00:20, and having time for a first-down-pass/spike package;
- same situation, at 00:15 and having time only for a boundary pass;
- not getting there with a 2nd-down play, seeing 00:20, 00:19, and having time only for an end zone pass;
- not getting there with a 1st-down play, seeing 00:46, 00:45, and having time for
    - a regular play and a spike;
    - a first-down pass and, if it is incomplete, another first-down pass and a spike;
    - a first-down pass and, if it is complete, a boundary pass, or
    - two boundary passes.
- not being sure that you have gotten to the field-goal line with a 3rd-down play, seeing 00:20, 00:19 and, decisively, either letting FG personnel hurry on or calling for an end zone pass;
- getting there with a 3rd-down play but being short of a first down, seeing 00:22, 00:21, and having to do a 4th-down hurry-on of FG personnel.
- reaching field-goal distance with a 2nd-down play, seeing 00:20, 00:19, and being able to do a spike to stop the clock to get FG personnel on;
- getting there with a first down at 00:03 and spiking;
- same situation at 00:02 and throwing an end zone pass;
- getting there, seeing 00:19, 00:18, wanting to spike but being afraid of time going to 00:02, calling for an end-zone-pass/spike package, and having the QB go for the end zone if he does not see 00:03 or more at the snap;
- getting there with a 3rd-down play, seeing 00:37, 00:36, and being able to bleed away all but four seconds before a 4th-down kick;
- getting there with a 2nd-down play, seeing 00:37, 00:36, and being able to bleed time before a 3rd-down spike;
- getting there with a one-point lead and a sure FG, knowing how many time-outs your opponent has, and needing to keep him from letting you score;
- getting there, seeing 00:35, 00:34, not wanting to pass, not having time to penult with a run, hurrying on the FG personnel, and bleeding;

In order for players to do clock offense well, they must have practiced in the stadium with the scoreboard clock.

- getting there with a first down, seeing 00:35, running, then spiking;
- getting there with 2nd-and-eight on the 18, seeing 00:44, 00:43, wanting only to run, running, then spiking;
- getting there, seeing 00:20, 00:19, wanting a 4th-down hurry-on but running short of time and trying to rattle the play-caller or the QB into the mistake of a 4th-down spike.
- getting there, with a 1st-down play, seeing 00:35, 00:34, calling for a first-down-pass/spike package, getting sacked, and having only an end-zone pass,
- getting there, seeing 00:19, 00:18, getting lined up for a FG on 3rd down, bleeding, fumbling the snap and, having no time for a 4th-down kick, yelling for the impromptu moveout pass;
- getting there, seeing 00:26, 00:25, getting lined up for a FG on 3rd down, bleeding, fumbling the snap, having time for a 4th-down kick, and executing a quick incomplete pass;
- being there barely, seeing 00:32, 00:31 on 3rd-and-10, and having time for the no sack/hold/interception pass for a first down and a spike, with FG position assured if the pass is incomplete;
- not getting there, seeing 00:15, 00:14 as a play ends, and trying to execute an end-zone pass;
- trying to get to the FG line, which is five yards short of the first-down line, having time for a hurry-on but surprisingly getting a first down with about 00:22, throwing a first-down pass, spiking, and kicking;
- getting to the FG line at 00:36, 00:35, with a 2nd-down play, having 00:21, 00:20 for a first-down pass, hitting it, spiking at 00:06, 00:05, stopping the clock at 00:03, and kicking;
- not getting to the first-down line or the FG line, seeing 00:22, 00:21 on 4th down, and having to throw for the end zone.

Along the way, have the QB experience

- having to change a regular play to a first-down pass, a first-down pass to a boundary pass, a boundary pass to an end-zone pass, and a spike to an end-zone pass;
- having an end-zone-pass/spike package called on a 1st or 2nd down, and spiking only if the ball can be snapped with 00:03;
- bleeding time before (a) a 4th-down kick, (b) a time-out, (c) a spike and (d) a 4th-down play, and
- not being sure that the FG line has been reached, going ahead and signaling the clock formation, looking for the play signal, and letting himself be interrupted by a hurry-on.

Case: Penn State and Indiana are tied at 00:51, 00:50. Penn State has the ball on the Indiana 25, with 2nd-and-two and no time-outs. Can they execute two more runs before kicking? The barriers for penults are for stopped, first-down, and moving clocks. The problem is to think ahead to what the clock might read after this 2nd-down play. (1) A stopped clock will allow plenty of time to think. (2) A first-down clock at about 00:30 will leave time for a run that does not stop the clock and a hurry-on. (3) A moving clock, at about 00:32, 00:31, will leave time only for a first-down pass at about 00:15, 00:14 and an incomplete pass or a spike. The only way to have two runs is to get a first down or an out-of-bounds on one of them. Penn State gets a first down on the 21, does not get in a second play, kicks, and wins.

For two examples of scripting and one of reciting thoughts see Appendix M.

Comparing Kinds of Plays

In comparing plays that will leave the three kinds of clocks, it is useful to think of the time needed for a regular play as the time needed for (a) two first-down passes, if one of them is incomplete, or (b) two boundary passes:

- 00:25   regular penult
- 00:16, 00:15   ref begins his process
- 00:01   final kick or play

- 00:25   first-down pass, incomplete
- 00:15   first-down pass and 20 seconds (including the ref's time) for a hurry-on kick or 00:05 for a play

- 00:25   boundary pass
- 00:15   boundary pass
- 00:05   final kick or play

Thinking beyond the Next Play

Imagine yourself needing a FG to win, and being three yards short of the FG line and six yards short of the first-down line, with 3rd-and-six and 00:26, stopped. You plan to run to the FG line, have 00:20, 00:19, hurry FG personnel on, and kick. You must also allow for (1) not getting to the FG line and for (2) getting to the first-down line. If (1), you will call an end-zone pass. If (2), and you see 00:20, you have time for a first-down pass and a spike. If (2) and you see 00:15, you have time only for a boundary pass. Again, thinking ahead is what makes this so difficult.

Reviewing Last-Ditch Possibilities Out of a Moving Clock

This is what there is time for, out of a moving clock, when you are out of time-outs:

- 00:16, 00:15   some hope for the ball to be ready for one final snap,
- 00:21, 00:20   a hurry-on if you have made the FG line, or an end-zone pass if you have not, or any final play,
- 00:26, 00:25   a hurry-on if you have made the FG line, or a boundary pass if you have not,
- 00:31, 00:30   a hurry-on if you have made the FG line, or a first-down pass and a spike if you have not,
- 00:46, 00:45   a regular play and either a hurry-on or a final play.

Going for a TD with or without a Time-Out

Earlier it was established that the average time consumed by a play in stop-the-clock offense is about 15 seconds and the number of passing plays that can be executed in a given amount of time at twice the number of running plays. Also, a way to compute the yardage that needs to be gained per play was explained.

Going for a TD is mostly procedural. Going for a FG is more decisional. For a TD you get in as many plays as you can and finish by going for the end zone. Because you can go for a TD without distance being as critical, because you can throw two or three times for the end zone, and because you use time-outs exclusively to add plays, decisions are limited to

- running for the end zone once or passing several times,
- either using up excess time or considering only the percentage chance of scoring, and
- trying to squeeze in a penult, exactly as you do for a FG, or just going for the end zone twice.

Because a time-out is used to add plays and not to protect a final play, there is no reason to discuss, separately, driving with and without one. What you do is have the play-caller practice in three types of decisions:

1. Bring him down the field to a 1st-and-goal on the two with 00:18 and let him choose between three end-zone passes or one run.

2. Bring him inside the 20 with different numbers of time-outs (yours and your opponent's) and, consequently, different problems in excess clock time.

3. Bring him to FG-type penult decisions and let him choose (a) a penult and a final play or (b) a final play and, if time remains, another final play.

Practicing on the Field

In walk-throughs and even in sit-throughs with chairs as defenders, do all signals and pointings. In individual work with position coaches, enact FAST play, especially for backs and ends.

> ***You do not want a clock embarrassment to expose a lack of preparation.***

In pass-skeleton work, assemble all parts of clock passing. The organizational problems are with the clock operator, the scripted ball-spotter, and the acting officials. The small scoreboard-like stopwatch can be held in front of the QB's face to take the place of a scoreboard clock. In frontal work, practice all parts of clock running, from an out-of-bounds sweep to the play to take a safety.

For conditioning work, execute a play every 20 seconds against a cooperating defense, with WRs substituting themselves after deep routes have been run. Do fifteen plays in five minutes, and conditioning will have taken place.

For fulfillment, go to the stadium and enact clock football. To accumulate offensive experience, you have to follow a script and have at least three coaches telling defenders how to play. In truly competitive work you will not get to enough of the situations that you must experience.

For thoroughness for coaches and QBs, go back to the indoor simulator. Requisite reps can be achieved only there.

For efficiency and proficiency, practice enough so that clock pressure will not affect execution. Often it does.

Case: Northwestern is behind Indiana by two in the second quarter, with three time-outs and 01:56. Screw-ups are ahead. First, Northwestern returns a punt to the IU 8 but blocks illegally and gets put back to their own 18—a 74 yard swing. Second, they waste a time-out after getting a first down. Third, the QB gets called for intentional grounding. Fourth, a receiver runs out-of-bounds a yard short of the first down line when he could have stayed inbounds, bulled his way to the line, and stopped the clock.

Case: Minnesota and Purdue are tied at the end of the second quarter. Minnesota drives and gets a first down on the Purdue 44, with 00:29 and three time-outs. They should get in four snaps, maybe five. What happens? (1) They use one time-out on a first down. (2) They use another because of an organizational problem. (3) They have the clock stopped for a penalty and do not get the ball snapped for six seconds after the ready signal. (4) They hit a pass on the 35, leaving 4th-and-one and 00:00.

21

Playing Clock Defense

Playing Against Your Opponent's Stop-the-Clock Offense

If your offense is going to be able to consume the remaining time, you do not want an interceptor, on a 1st, 2nd, or 3rd down, to try to run and, in trying, fumble. Pass defenders can put themselves on alert by communicating, like baseball players, back and forth: "On an interception, get to the ground." This means that an interceptor is to get to the ground without getting tackled.

A potential interceptor on a 4th down wants to turn down an interception; he wants to smash the ball to the ground. Why? Because it is safer. Pass defenders can communicate with: "Fourth down. Don't intercept. Smash the ball."

On a last-down Hail Mary a potential interceptor is in danger of either deflecting the ball to an offender or being involved in a simultaneous catch that would go to the offender. He definitely wants to smash the ball.

> *If a defender gets an interception when time remaining will let his QB just fall on the ball, he should get to the ground, not run.*

Case: Pittsburgh, up by 7 over Virginia Tech in the fourth quarter, gets the ball at 03:39. They bleed and give the ball back at 00:39. In those last seconds, (a) a Pitt defender tries, unsuccessfully, to pick up a fumble instead of falling on it and ending the game, (b) a Pitt DB tries to compete for a Hail Mary pass and lets it be completed instead of being smashed to the ground, and (c) a Pitt rusher roughs the passer on the Hail Mary pass. Pitt wins anyway.

An injured player wants to get off the field without the Ref stopping the clock and giving the offense time to communicate.

Tacklers near sidelines want to work to keep ballcarriers from fighting their way out-of-bounds.

To delay the process of getting the ball ready for play, defenders want to pursue, gang tackle, and unpile reluctantly. Officials are not supposed to let themselves be delayed, but defenders want to try, anyway.

If you are behind by one or even tied and the opponent is in position for an easy field goal and threatening to leave you no time to answer, you want to consider letting him score. His seven points could leave you some hope of returning the kickoff, scoring eight or seven, and getting to overtime.

To keep your opponent from running the ball, you can attack gaps, grab frontal receivers, play without a safety, and compress the front so you can have protected backside linebackers.

Mostly, you play defense to stop the kinds of plays he must execute in order to get the points he needs. Mostly, you determine how many yards he needs to make per play, and then you set your defense.

On the low side and roughly, you can figure a consumption of five seconds for each play for which the opponent has a time-out and an average of 10 seconds for other plays. Roughly, you can divide the number of plays he can execute in the time-remaining into the yards he has to make, and you can get the yards he has to make per play. Roughly, you can anticipate what he is going to be trying to do to you. Roughly, you can say something like,

- "We can let them have the short passes and the runs that will keep the clock moving." Or,
- "We've got to stop 20-yard passes." Or,
- "We've got to stop first-down passes." Or,
- "We've got to keep a strong run defense."

It is only when he has a 1st-and-goal and is assured of time to execute all four of his plays that you can use your time-outs to save time for yourself without saving time for him.

Playing Against His Move-the-Clock Offense

You can use time-outs on the plays where your opponent tries to consume seconds, and you can save for yourself 40 seconds per time-out.

Case: Tennessee is behind LSU 6-24 in the second quarter. They have two time-outs and have forced an LSU punt. LSU consumes 48 seconds with its 4th-down punt. Tennessee starts with 01:34, having lost as many as seven clock-stopping plays by not using a time-out. Later, Tennessee gets a first down on the +19 with 00:16 and gets off only one more play—a completed pass that could not stop the clock, because it was for less than a first down.

To speed up the process of getting the ball ready for play, defenders can unpile quickly and get lined up.

Case: Georgia Tech is ahead of Maryland 17-14 in the fourth quarter. Tech has a first down on their own 36, with 03:02. Maryland will win in overtime. How? (1) They use all three time-outs on the Tech offense. After Tech gets a first down, they save their last time-out for the 2nd-down so it will save more time. (2) They get a Tech runner to go out-of-bounds, which saves them 40 seconds. (3) Then, from the Tech 28 with 3rd-and-10 and 00:15, they throw a first-down pass, spike, kick, and tie.

When the QB is going to take a knee, defensive linemen can attack both shoulders of the center and try to knock him into the QB, giving them their only chance to create a fumble.

When the QB is going to sweep to bleed time, a containing end-of-the-line defender can keep him from doing it.

Case: Michigan is up by 10 over Utah, as the second quarter nears its end. Utah starts on its 20, with 00:33. Michigan has three time-outs and uses them. Utah punts, with 00:10. Because Michigan has been careful, they should get one shot at the end zone. They rough the Utah punter, however, and never get that shot. The point here: Defenders who stop offenders need time-outs to stop the clock.

Playing Against an Opponent's Extra-Period Offense

In an extra period, if your offense has already had the ball, you can use your one time-out to "ice" his FG kicker. If there is to be no FG, you can use it to coach your defense for the final play.

22

Sustaining Progress

Noting a Lack of Preparation

The real-life cases included here expose a lack of preparation.

Programs must lack (a) ways to practice indoors, on table-tops, with high repetitions and (b) scripts for insuring thoroughness. There must not be clock-management specialists who can hold cards with the numbers that are needed to support the management.

At clinics, football books on display have not one good chapter on clock management. In two wonderful books about offense, by Super Bowl heroes, there is almost nothing.

From the booth in a televised college game, one hears, with the dropping of a first-down pass in a clock drive:

"It is just as well that the receiver dropped the ball, because it was thrown over the middle."

From coaches, one hears talk about players not having experience, maturity, size, speed, and play-making ability. Never is there any talk about coaches not having preparation for clock management.

Case: Leading Pittsburgh 13-7 in the second quarter, Miami drives almost the length of the field and dies on the two-inch line. They had wasted a time-out because of confusion and wasted a down by spiking on a 1st-and-goal. To make two inches they needed only the time and the down that they had wasted.

Recognizing an Analogy

There is not a metaphor for this subject. There is, however, an analogy. It is in aviation in emergency procedures, where simulation is standard practice.

1. In neither, can you wait to learn from experience.
2. In both, you must have indoor simulation.
3. In either, if you cannot think clearly, you can be quickly overwhelmed.
4. In both, you must know, ahead of time, what you will do if certain things happen.
5. In both, proficiency requires continuing practice.
6. In both, you need help—on a sideline from a clock-management specialist, in a cockpit from a co-pilot or an air-traffic controller.
7. In both, you must be ready to respond to emergencies you will never face.
8. In neither, can you make a major mistake and survive.

Working in Your Laboratory

You cannot go to many games. You cannot get many tapes of games. When you watch games on TV, you cannot see much of what is happening on the field. You cannot go to many clinics. You cannot own many books.

You can, however, study clock management in the "laboratory" of your own TV room. All of the information that you need—down-and-distance, ball-position, score, kind of clock, time-remaining, time-outs, action of the ref—is on the screen. Furthermore, you can do it competitively, trying to conceptualize problems better than the booth and make decisions better than the coach.

- "Okay," you might say, with eyes on the screen, "with no time-outs and eighteen seconds on the first-down clock, the coach can throw into the end zone three times or run for the goal line once."
- Or, "Now, with forty-six, forty-five on the moving clock, there can be a quick third-down run that does not stop the clock and a hurry-on of field-goal personnel."

You need a columnized writing pad. You also need your own shorthand and symbols, so you can notate without looking down.

You want to put down, as a play ends, the following: kind of play, time as the play ends, kind of clock, down-and-distance, yard line, and time of the next snap. As you write you want to say, out loud, what you would do. This way, you can experience the drive and, then, go back and critique it.

When possible, you want to tape the last four minutes of second and fourth quarters that might have clock-management problems.

Having an Indoor Practice Space Ready

Imagine a visitor coming upon your practice space and looking around.

- On the wall there is a writing board for coaching, a pin board for informing, and framed items for inspiring; on two tables and a shelf, there are paraphernalia.
- Pinned on the board are (a) a roster of players for signing off by coaches on readiness for clock offense; (b) a list of managers for signing off on individual readiness to operate the stadium clock during clock work; (c) a survey that shows where each coach and QB places his watersheds on the tough decisions; (d) grades from oral and written tests; (e) dates for upcoming clock events, like a visit by a real referee; (f) an agenda for progressing; (g) a cartoon of a QB walking with an adoring girl, with a cloud above him showing his thoughts, which are about clock offense.
- Framed are (a) lines from play-by-play sheets that document past clock-management successes; (b) a picture of the team on the field doing something impressive in a drive, with an inset of the scoreboard clock; (c) a picture of the play-caller in the pressbox with the arms of his distance-to-go man looped around his head; and (d) a picture of the sideline, with a hand-signal being delivered.
- Laminated and lying on one of the tables are (a) the pointing assignments for all plays, (b) checklists for simulated drives, (c) a summary of rules that the clock evokes, (d) tests that players are going to have to take, and (e) questions that each QB must answer, alone in a room, in front of a video camera.
- On a shelf are (a) handbooks and (b) video tapes with segments from televised college games showing clock management.
- On the other table are a green football-field board, two stopwatches, mini-markers for positions of the chains and the ball, and five chairs. In a corner are more green boards, ready to be borrowed.

Testing Your Readiness

You are behind, 19-21, in the fourth quarter. Your time-outs are gone. A 3rd-down play has just left you two feet short of the first-down line and five feet short of the field-goal line. A moving clock shows 00:38, 00:37. What do you do? It is 4th down. You have two seconds to decide.

Do you hurry-on field-goal personnel and kick from farther away than you wanted? Do you throw a boundary pass past the FG line and, if you hit it, kick and, if you do not, lose? Do you just go for the FG line and, if you make it, spike and kick and, if you do not, lose? Do you just go for the first-down line? Do you just go for the end zone to be certain that the game ends with the ball in the end zone? Whatever you do will spell the end of the game.

Until you have confronted such a situation in simulation and have practiced deciding without hesitating, you are not ready for a game.

Closing with Reasons for this Effort

Why study and practice for clock management? You do it because

- you have as much natural ability for it as anyone,
- it is the same problem at all levels,
- the clock plays no favorites, so it is not who you know but what you know,
- it is the same problem in all years, so your learning will never be out-of-date,
- it is difficult and, while clock management is not rocket science, rocket science is not clock management,
- to teach it to a QB is to make him smart, and a young person wants most to be made to be smart,
- if you want to get tested, you will; if you do not want to run out of things to learn, you will not; and, if you want to look smart, you can,
- ten thousand guys are working on offense and defense, while only a few are working on clock management,
- when the pressure is on, when a great player wants to control the ball, a great coach wants to control the clock.

Appendices

Appendix A

Case: Alabama vs. North Texas State, second quarter, 01:59, Alabama's ball on the + 48, one time-out. Later: Alabama, 3rd-and-goal on the five, last time-out called at 00:17. Now, they can only throw. Could they have saved enough seconds to make a run possible? On one first down—loss of 3; on another first down—loss of 13; between a 2nd and a 3rd down—loss of 23. That is 39 seconds. Yes, they could have made a 3rd-and-goal run possible.

Case: Late in the fourth quarter Appalachian State is down by three to Montana. Wisely, they use their last time-out on a Montana punt and start on their 19 with 02:44. They are going to squander 34 seconds, be forced to kick to tie, and lose in overtime. Here is where the 34 seconds went:

- Snap at 02:44. First down. Next snap at 02:22. Loss of 15.
- Later, snap at 02:14. Plus two. Next snap at 01:46. Loss of eight.
- Later, snap at 01:26. First down. Next snap at 01:18. Loss of three.
- Later, 28 seconds elapse between plays. Loss of eight.

And Appalachian State was playing for a shot at the national championship.

Case: Central Florida is behind Alabama 37-38 in the fourth quarter. They are on their own 21, with 02:15 and no time-outs. They hustle to each new LOS and show no hesitation or confusion. At the Alabama 20, they spike, kick, and win. But the kick was on a 2nd down. Could they have saved time for one more run? Let us see. The second play of their drive starts 28 seconds after the first. A first down stops the clock at 01:21, and the 1st-down play starts at 01:14. The next play starts 30 seconds later. A first down stops the clock at 00:34, and the next snap is at 00:31. They could have saved eight, six, 10, and two seconds—26 in all. Time for one more run? Yes. Still, they get their victory.

Case: Texas Tech needs a TD to beat Nebraska. They have the ball, 4th-and-six, on the +35. They have three time-outs, and they call one. The booth had suggested that they should call one. Time-outs are for adding plays and, if Nebraska takes over while still ahead, Tech is going to want all three. Nebraska does take over and gets a FG at 03:25. Now Tech needs a TD and a FG. With possession of the ball they continue to huddle and get plays from the sideline. Also, they lose a total of 35 seconds after three first downs. Tech's management of the clock has defeat written all over it, and they lose the game.

Case: Boston College is seven points ahead of Army in the second quarter. They have the ball, 1st-and-10 on their 16, with 01:23. They will execute 11 plays brilliantly and, after a questionable call at the end line, settle for a FG. The booth, after a first down was made on an out-of-bounds play: "That's good to get out-of-bounds, so they won't have to burn a time-out." BC did make one questionable move. With that first down and 00:34 on Army's 21 and needing a FG, they use one of two time-outs. They are in FG range and want one time-out to get FG personnel on after a 3rd-down run. That left none for after the 1st or 2nd down, when the clock could have been moving.

Appendix B

Diagram B-1 shows the pointing assignment for a counter off-tackle.

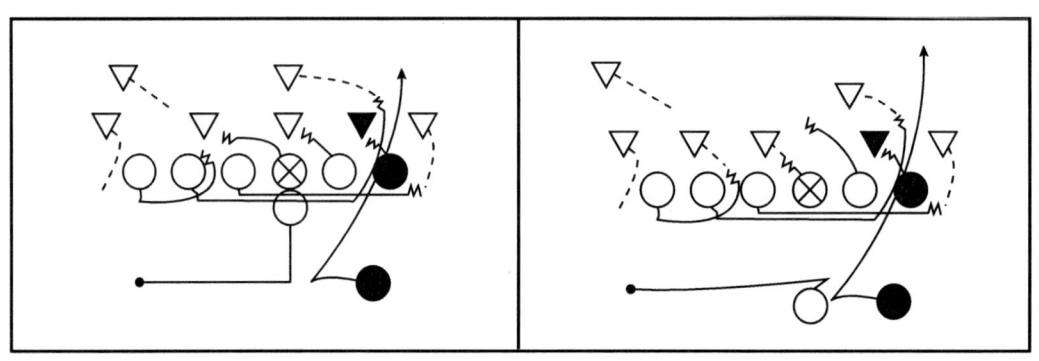

Diagram B-1a and b

Diagram B-2 shows the pointing assignment for a sprintout run-or-pass.

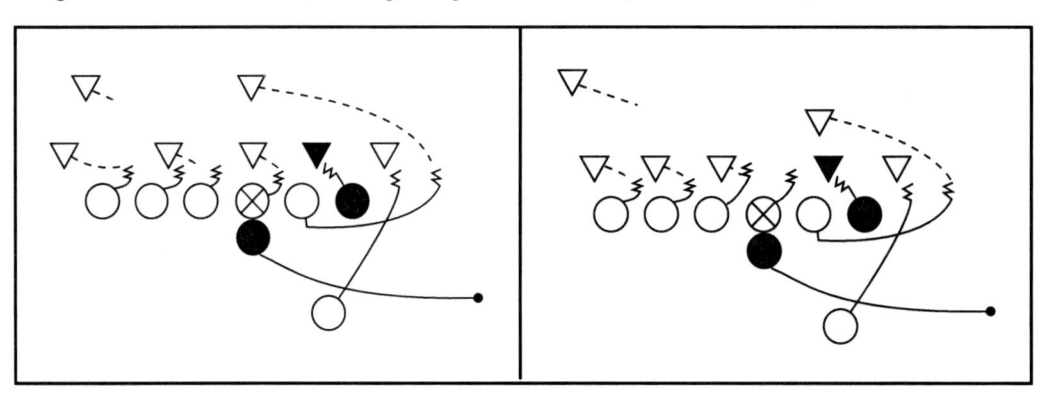

Diagram B-2a and b

Diagram B-3 shows the pointing assignment for a trap.

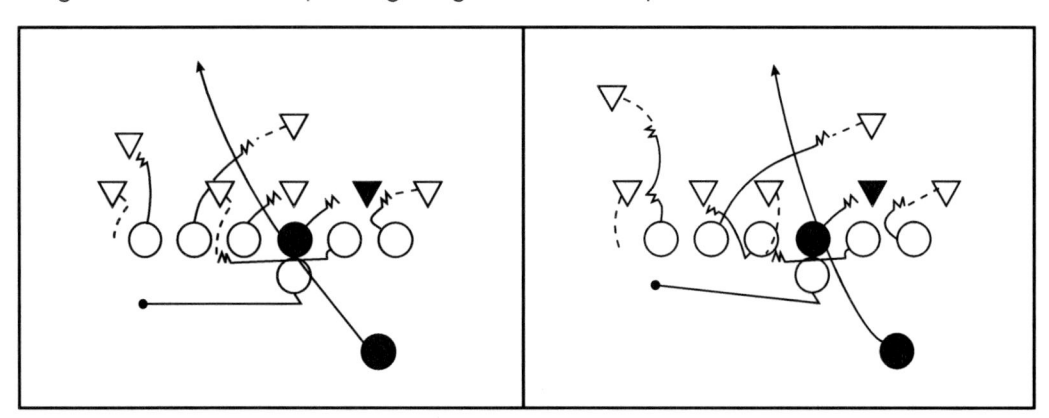

Diagram B-3a and b

Appendix C

Case: Georgia is ahead of Tennessee 5-0 in the second quarter, with two time-outs, the ball on the +36, and 00:38. They waste a time-out with the clock stopped, by the old rule, for change of possession. They use their last time-out wisely and go on to a first down on the Tennessee 22 at 00:13. With the time-out that they wasted, they could run, get closer, call the time-out, and kick. As it is, they have to spike. They make the field goal anyway.

Case: Wisconsin is behind Northern Illinois by four, late in the fourth quarter. They use two of three time-outs on the NIU offense. When they get the ball, they use their last at 01:40. The booth says they called it too soon. But they need a TD, not a FG, and all that the one time-out can do is add plays. Called at 01:40 or at 00:20, all it can do is add plays. You want to call it, add the plays, and know exactly what time you have left.

Case: Vanderbilt is giving Alabama fits in the second quarter. Alabama punts from deep in its own territory, after letting the clock go down to 00:42. Vandy did not have a time-out by which to save 40 seconds. Vandy goes to Alabama's 36 and has 00:33. They throw incomplete and, then, complete at 00:21. They spike, and the clock stops at 00:05. The spike probably costs them a play. Not having just one time-out to use on Alabama's punt did cost them as many as five or six plays.

Case: Fresno State, ranked tenth nationally, is down by five to Boise State. They start on their 20, with 03:55 left in the game and all three time-outs. The booth: "Four-down status." No. Not with three time-outs. Fresno gets to a 4th-and-8 on the Boise 20. Time-out. Penalty. Another time-out. The booth suggests, "If Fresno fails on the 4th down, Boise can take a knee." No. Fresno has one time-out. Boise calls time-out at 01:38. They want time to get a FG if Fresno gets a TD. Wise? Tough call. Fresno fails. Boise takes over, takes a knee, and takes the win.

Appendix D

Fourth quarter, going in to score a TD and win, ball on the +19, 01:59, a stopped clock, 2nd-and-10, two time-outs. You need 55 seconds inside the 10 to be able to use all four of your downs. You must score but you would like to leave your opponent minimum time for an answer. Do you consider only the down-and-distance in choosing between a run and a pass, *or* do you run until you can expect to have approximately those 55 seconds?

Second quarter, behind by seven, ball on your opponent's 11, 05:13, 05:12, two time-outs, 4th-and-three. Do you take a sure three points, kick off and count on stopping him and driving for a TD, *or* do you try for a first down, maybe go on to get a touchdown and, if you fail, leave him deep in his own territory with you still behind by seven?

Fourth quarter, behind by two, ball on your opponent's 39, no time-outs, clock stopped at 00:09, 2nd-and-10. Do you throw a boundary pass, then an end-zone pass, *or* do you throw two end-zone passes?

Fourth quarter, your opponent's ball on your 29, 2nd-and-10, 00:44, 00:43. He is down by two and has no time-outs. You have three time-outs. Do you let him run once and try about a 42-yard field goal, *or* do you use your time-outs, let him run twice, and hope to have about 30 seconds to answer with a FG in case he makes a FG?

You are playing a superior opponent. You have 182 yards; the opponent has 412. You score to get within one point, with 00:08 left in the game. Do you kick and try to win in an extra period *or* do you gamble now on making two points, going ahead, stopping his kickoff return, and winning?

You score to go up by two. There are 11 seconds left in the game. Do you kick, to go up by three, *or* do you take a knee?

It is the fourth quarter, with 03:48 left. You have the ball on your 26, 4th-and-one. You are down by four and have all three time-outs. Do you punt, use your time-outs on your opponent's offense, and count on him punting and you being able to drive, *or* do you go for the yard? Tough call.

Fourth quarter, need a FG from the 22 to win, ball on the 29, 3rd-and-five, 00:28, 00:27, no time-outs. Your barrier for a first-down pass and a spike is 00:30; for a boundary pass, 00:25. To get to the 22, do you throw for the first down and count on spiking, *or* do you throw for a boundary?

Appendix E

Down by 10 in the fourth quarter, you are starting on your 39, with 10:41 and three time-outs. You have the offensive team around you with a few seconds to say, "Hustle mode. Stay on the line unless Kevin calls for a huddle. Get out-of-bounds if you do not have a first down. Stay in and get more yards if you do. We save our time-outs to use on the opponent's offense."

Just before halftime, with the score tied, your opponent is punting from his 22. You have your QB beside you, and you say, "We're going to take over at about our forty with about a minute forty. We have two time-outs, but check with the white cap to verify that. Tell the guys we're in a hustle mode. I'll signal if I want to change. Let's try for a touchdown but settle for a field goal from the twenty. Use the time-outs as you need them, but if you still have one when you get to the twenty, save it for the field goal."

You are down by one with the ball on your 25, 01:20 on a stopped clock, and no time-outs. You say to your QB, "Tell 'em we're playing fast to get the field goal. Be ready for a third-down spike or a fourth-down hurry-on. Remember: With forty-five on a moving clock or thirty-five on a first-down clock, you can do a penult and either spike on a third or hurry-on on a fourth. If we don't get to the twenty-five, we want our last play to be an end-zone pass."

It is almost halftime. You have been trying for a TD, but it is 3rd-and-10 on the +18, right hash, with 00:10 on a clock stopped by your second time-out. You say to your QB, "Let's get a field goal. One more run off-tackle and you are in the ref's face to call time-out even if you get a first down. Tell Rodney to stay in front of the goalposts, no zigging and zagging no matter what he sees."

You need a TD. The clock is stopped at 01:05. You are on the opponent's 17, with one time-out. You say to your QB, "We're in fast play. As long as you have that time-out, I can call anything as a penult and you can get in the white cap's face and call time-out. Remember, if you are at the line and you are not going to have at least eight seconds on a moving clock for the penult, you forget it, let the clock go down to four, and call the time-out."

It is the fourth quarter, and you need a TD to win. It appears that you will be taking a punt between your 40 and the 50. You will have one time-out and about 01:50. You have your quarterback in front of you. You say, "Fast play. Tell 'em we'll need every second we can save. It's all passes, unless it's fourth-and-short. Use the time-out when you have to. Picture the barriers for penults—after a first down, thirty-five, twenty, and fifteen, and with the clock moving, forty-five, thirty-five, and thirty."

You just got an interception and have the ball on your opponent's 18, with 01:21 left in the first half, down by one. You grab your QB. "We'll keep it on the ground and take a field goal if it goes to fourth down. We're out of time-outs, so remember the barriers for the clock-stopping penults—thirty, fifteen, and ten. A hurry-on is for fourth down. A spike package is for first or second down."

You have got to get a TD from your 36, without a time-out. You have 01:13. About to start your drive, you are instructing your QB. "We're out of time-outs, so we're throwing only boundary and first-down passes. Remind the receivers about first-down depths. With thirty-five on a moving clock or twenty on a first-down clock, we can get a first down and then throw for the end zone. If thirty or fifteen, we go boundary and then end zone."

You are just past the line for the FG that you need to win. It is second down. You just burned your last time-out, at 00:52. To your QB: "We'll probably have to hurry on. After this play we can get in one more inbounds play as long as we have forty-five on a moving clock. I may fudge a little."

Tied, you take over on your 36 in the second quarter, with 01:59 left and one time-out. To your QB: "Let's play fast and stay on the line even when the clock stops. The defense feels the pressure. If we fall behind schedule and I want to change to deliberate play to consume time, I'll signal you. Use that time-out as soon as you need it."

You are backed up before the half, with 03:23 and three time-outs. You say to your QB: "Let's do deliberate play until we get to midfield, then you can go fast. Let's not save the opponent time for his offense. Tell the guys that right now we're just putting first downs together."

Second quarter. You are on your opponent's 41 and need to get to the 20 to kick. A stopped clock shows 00:38. Time-outs are gone. It is 2nd-and-10. You say to your QB: "We need 20 more yards. I'll call first-down passes, until we have to go to the boundary. Remember, you can throw a boundary penult if you are going to get the snap with nine seconds. If you see eight, yell for and signal for an end-zone pass."

Appendix F

Case: Pittsburgh ties Syracuse 17-17, with 01:17 left. Syracuse starts back with two time-outs and a first down on their 17. After intentional grounding puts them on their four, with 2nd-and-23, they go first down, first down, time-out, 2nd-and-three at 00:30. Run. Now, 00:28, 00:27. There is time to start another play at 00:13, 00:12 and get closer before calling the last time-out. But they do not do it. Their kick is from too far away. In an extra period, Syracuse wins anyway.

Case: Auburn, against Wyoming, is trying to get a FG before the half. They have one time-out. Suddenly, they have a first down on the +28, with 00:17. They can pass or run to a boundary, run to gain some yardage and position the ball, call time-out, and kick. If a boundary run does not stop the clock, they have the time-out. Somehow, the ball is not snapped until 00:10. The one play fails, time-out is called, and the kick misses.

Case: Behind Florida by two, Georgia recovers a fumble on the Florida five, with 01:11. There are four runs in that time. The clock is stopped. The first run will take 10 seconds, the second 25, the third 25, and the fourth, after a time-out, one. Georgia does not do it exactly this way, but they get to their 4th down and kick a field goal. This is after suffering a five-yard penalty on the 2nd down.

Appendix G

Case: Mississippi State scores, gets within five (12-17) of Mississippi, goes for two, misses, and stays behind by five. MSU had a card that said to go for two when behind by five in order to have a chance to be behind by three; to go for two because being behind by five is not significantly worse than being behind by four. This card is for when the remaining scoring is all expected to be by the team that is behind. It is not for when the other team may very well score. Follow the reason why:

1. If Ole Miss gets a FG, it will be 12-20, and MSU will wish they had kicked so they would be behind by seven rather than eight.

2. If Ole Miss gets a TD, it will be 12-24, and MSU will wish they had kicked so they would be behind by 11 rather than 12.

3. If MSU gets a TD and Ole Miss gets a FG, it will be 19-20, and MSU will wish they had kicked so they would be tied.

4. If MSU gets a FG and Ole Miss gets a TD, it will be 15-24, and they will wish they had kicked so they would be behind by eight rather than nine.

5. If MSU gets a TD and a FG and Ole Miss gets a TD, it will be 22-24, and they will be happy that they went for two and at least took a chance at having 24.

In only one of the situations above would MSU be happy that they went for two, even though they failed.

Case: North Carolina State goes ahead of Minnesota 31-27 early in the fourth quarter, goes for two, and misses. Smart? No. Only if Minnesota answers with a field goal will it be smart. The possible scores after NCS goes ahead are 31-27, 32-27, and 33-27. If Minnesota answers with a TD, NCS wants to be behind by only two (32-34), not three (31-34). If NCS gets a FG, they want to be ahead by eight (35-27), not seven (34-27); if a TD, 12 (39-27), not 11 (38-27). Only if Minnesota answers with a FG and NCS is left ahead by one, after missing the two-pointer, would going for two look smart. They would have taken a chance at being ahead by three and lost nothing by turning down a chance to be ahead by two and leaving themselves ahead by one. NCS wins by eight (38-30). They would have been safer ahead by nine (39-30).

Case: Mississippi State scores against Mississippi in the second quarter to get within two, 12-14. Minus 2 is on the card but there will be more scoring. They try for a two-pointer and fail. Will they regret trying? Let us see. Mississippi scores and MSU goes down by 9, 12-21. Would MSU rather be down by 8? Yes. Next, MSU kicks a FG to make it 15-21. Now they are down by 6. Would it make a difference to be down by 5? Not much. Next, MSU scores and goes ahead 22-21. Would they rather be 23-21? Not especially. Next, MSU scores again, kicks for one and goes up 29-21, by 8. Would they rather be ahead by 9? Yes. Next, MSU scores again and kicks. It is 36-21, ahead by 15. Would they rather be ahead by 16? Yes. Next Mississippi scores, kicks, and gets within 8, 36-28. Would MSU rather be up by 9? Yes.

Appendix H

Each of these additions of points, after your subtraction of two points, makes it regrettable that you subtracted two. The first number is your points if a safety is not taken; the second is your points if one is taken.

You are ahead, +6 goes to +4:

- Add the opponent's FG   +3 / +1
- Add his two FGs   0 / −2
- Add his TD   -1 / -3
- Add his two TDs   −8 / −10
- Add your FG   +9 / +7
- Add your two FGs   +12 / +10
- Add your TD   +13 / +11
- Add your two TDs   +20 / +18

You are behind, −4 goes to −6:

- Add the opponent's FG   −7 / −9
- Add his two FGs   −10 / −12
- Add his TD   −11 / −13
- Add his two TDs   −18 / −20
- Add your FG   −1 / −3
- Add your two FGs   +2 / 0
- Add your TD   +3 / +1
- Add your two TDs   +10 / +8

Appendix I

In comparing other scoring possibilities, there is always a two-point subtraction, and the result requires additional driving time, except when the subtraction leaves unchanged needs (+6 and +4 or −4 to −6).

The differentials from which you can subtract these other scoring possibilities and get + 6 and +4 are

- +13, from which −7 and −9 leaves +6 and +4,
- +11, from which −5 and −7 leaves +6 and +4, and
- +9, from which −3 and −5 leaves +6 and +4.

The differentials to get −4 and −6 are

- +3, from which −7 and −9 leaves −4 and −6,
- +1, from which −5 and −7 leaves −4 and −6, and
- −1, from which −3 and −5 leaves −4 and −6.

The idea here is that, if the differential is +13 and if you are allowing for a TD to be scored against you and are choosing between a punt and a safety, you can favor taking the safety because -7 and -9 leave unchanged needs at +6 and +4.

Or, if the differential is -1 and you are allowing for a FG and you are choosing between a punt and a safety, you can favor taking a safety because -3 and -5 leave unchanged needs at -4 and -6.

Appendix J

Listing Points Needed after Safeties

Shown are (a) point differences before and after your safety and (b) the change in your situation. No two results of taking a safety are alike.

- 0 to −2 / tie, to FG to win
- +1 to −1 / win, to FG to win
- +2 to 0 / win, to tie
- +3 to +1 / FG to tie you, to FG to beat you
- +4 to +2 / TD to beat you, to FG to beat you
- +5 to +3 / TD to beat you, to FG to tie you
- +6 to +4 / TD to beat you, to same TD to beat you
- +7 to +5 / TD to tie you, to TD to beat you
- +8 to +6 / TD and two-pointer to tie you, to TD to beat you
- +9 to +7 / TD and FG to beat you, to TD to tie you
- +10 to +8 / TD and FG to tie you, to TD and two-pointer to tie you
- +11 to +9 / FG, TD, and two-pointer to tie you, to FG and TD to beat you
- +12 to +10 / two TDs to beat you, to TD and FG to tie you
- +13 to +11 / two TDs to beat you, to FG, TD, and two-pointer to tie you
- +14 to +12 / two TDs to tie you, to two TDs to beat you
- +15 to +13 / two TDs and one two-pointer to tie you, to two TDs to beat you
- +16 to +14 / two TDs and two two-pointers to tie you, to two TDs to tie you
- −1 to −3 / FG to win, to FG to tie
- −2 to −4 / FG to win, to TD to win
- −3 to −5 / FG to tie, to TD to win
- −4 to −6 / TD to win, to same TD to win
- −5 to −7 / TD to win, to TD to tie
- −6 to −8 / TD to win, to TD and two-pointer to tie
- −7 to −9 / TD to tie, to TD and FG to win
- −8 to −10 / TD and two-pointer to tie, to TD and FG to tie
- −9 to −11 / TD and FG to win, to FG, TD, and two-pointer to tie
- −10 to −12 / TD and FG to tie/ to two TDs to win

- −11 to −13 / FG, TD, and two-pointer to tie, to two TDs to win
- −12 to −14 / two TDs to win, to two TDs to tie
- −13 to −15 / two TDs to win, to two TDs and one two-pointer to tie
- −14 to −16 / two TDs to tie, to two TDs and two two-pointers to tie
- −15 to −17 / two TDs and one two-pointer to tie, to two TDs and FG to tie

Appendix K

Comparing a Safety and a Punt in Resulting Needs

Where −2 and −3 seem to leave the same scoring need, you can look deeper for a reason to choose the safety or the punt.

To go from −5 to −7, from a safety, would leave you needing the same driving; to go from −2 to −4 would leave you needing more. To go from +7 to +5 would leave the opponent needing the same driving time; to go from +4 to +2 would leave him needing less. This is to say that taking a safety from −5 is not as much of a loss as taking one at −2, and that taking one at +7 is not as much as taking one at +4.

To go from −5 to −8, from your punt and your opponent's FG, would leave you needing the same driving time; to go from −1 to −4 would leave you needing more. To go from +8 to +5 would leave him needing the same driving; to go from +4 to +1 would leave him needing less.

These deeper considerations can help you decide in situations where comparative numbers do not. Other considerations than these always come first, however.

Appendix L

Case: Arizona State is ahead of San Diego State 10-7, with 04:10 in the fourth quarter, when they get the ball on their 37. After five plays only 50 seconds will be gone. Why? (1) They fail to take the 25-second counter down after a penalty. (2) A receiver goes out-of-bounds unnecessarily after making a first down. (3) They throw two passes that go incomplete. And (4) SDS uses a time-out. Anyway, SDS gets the ball with plenty of time, only to miss a field goal that would have moved them to overtime.

Case: Clemson is ahead of Wake Forest in the fourth quarter 31-24, with a first down on their 20 and 01:15 on a stopped clock. Wake Forest has a time-out. The table included in Chapter 18 says to keep the ball alive if the clock shows between 01:05 and 01:20 and the opponent has one time-out. (You especially need numbers when the time is in the range where either falling on the ball or going for a first down can be a serious mistake.) Clemson hands the ball off, unnecessarily. Wake Forest does not get its time-out called for 11 seconds and forfeits its chance to make Clemson punt. Now, Clemson takes a knee, lets the 25-second counter run out, takes a penalty, lets time expire after the ball is declared ready, and wins.

Case: Oklahoma State scores and goes ahead of favored Oklahoma 16-13, with 01:36 left in the fourth quarter. OU's drive fails. OSU takes over on the OU nine, with 01:09. OU's two time-outs will be called after the 1st- and 2nd-down plays. The clock will move after the 3rd-down play. It will stop after the 4th-down play. OU is going to get the ball back. But OSU wants to use up as much time as possible. The booth wants OSU to take a knee to see what OU will do with "their time-out situation." OSU unwisely takes a knee twice, and has the clock stopped twice. Then they actually take a time-out before their 4th-down play, and OU gets the ball deep in their territory, with 00:16. They can hit two passes and kick for a tie. But they are intercepted.

Case: Florida State, in protecting a 28-17 lead over Georgia Tech, snaps the ball on their final six plays with these times on the 25-second counter:

- :03
- :02
- :02
- :03
- :00   intentional delay penalty
- :03

Every QB, with a 25-second counter and a little practice, can learn to do this.

Appendix M

Scripting

You can prefabricate drives that will leave the play-caller with exactly the decision problem you want. He can call his plays, and the controller can force the result that is scripted. For example, to stop the clock, a run can go out-of-bounds or a pass can go incomplete. This method relieves the controller from having to create as he goes and relieves the play-caller from having to do more than one drive to get a particular experience.

Objective: Start with one time-out. Get to 1st-and-goal on the one-yard line with 00:18 but without the time-out, and maximize chances of getting a TD.

1st and 10: +29
    see: 00:52   call:
    snap: 00:50   result: plus eight, out-of-bounds

2nd and 2: +21
    see: 00:43   call:
    snap: 00:43   result: plus 16, holding

2nd and 12: +31
    see: 00:36   call:
    snap: 00:35   result: loss, minus five, time-out

3rd and 17: +36
    see: 00:27   call:
    snap: 00:27   result: plus 35, first down

1st and goal: +1
    see: 00:18   call:
    snap: 00:17   result: incomplete or out-of-bounds

2nd and goal: +1
    see: 00:12   call:
    snap: 00:12   result: incomplete or out-of-bounds

3rd and goal: +1

see: 00:06   call: run, because there is not time for an incomplete pass and a 4th-down play

snap: 00:06   result: touchdown

With 00:18 on a first-down clock, you got in two plays that stopped the clock, plus a third play.

In connection with this, have penalty choices that pose dilemmas. Let us say with 00:19 you need a TD and have no time-outs. You are offered 1st-and-five on the nine or 2nd-and-inches on the four. With the 1st-and-five you can have four end-zone passes. With the 2nd-and-inches, if you run and make it, you can have two end-zone passes but, if you run and do not make it, you are finished.

Scripting Backwards

You can script by creating a problem and building the script backwards, always showing the times the QB sees as plays end:

Objective: With time-outs gone, kick a FG from the 22, preceded by a first-down pass and a spike.

    kick good

    snap at   00:03

2nd-and-10: +22   00:03

    spike

    snap at   00:06

1st-and-10: +22   00:07

    gain of nine, clock stopped temporarily

    snap at   00:11

    a first-down-pass/spike package is invited

3rd-and-6: +31   00:26, 00:25

    loss of three, clock moving

    snap at   00:30

2nd-and-3: +28   00:44, 00:43

    gain of seven, clock moving

    snap at   00:49

1st-and-10: +35   00:51
   gain of 13, clock stopped temporarily
   snap at   00:58

1st-and-10: +48   00:59

Then you can turn it over and have a progression to the desired problem:

1st-and-10: +48   00:59
   snap at   00:58
   gain of 13, clock stopped temporarily

1st-and-10: +35   00:51
   snap at   00:49
   gain of seven, clock moving

2nd-and-3: +28   00:44, 00:43
   snap at   00:30
   loss of three, clock moving

3rd-and-6: +31   00:26, 00:25
   a first-down-pass/spike package is invited
   snap at   00:11
   gain of nine, clocked stopped temporarily

1st-and-10: +22   00:07
   snap at   00:06
   spike

2nd-and-10: +22   00:03
   snap at   00:03
   kick good

Reciting Thoughts In Planning Ahead

In simulation a pressbox play-caller can say what his choices will be after the completion of a play but say them before the execution of the play. He can do this to force thinking ahead.

- You need a FG and have two time-outs. The ball is on your opponent's 49. The FG line is the 23. The drive is underway. You have 00:34 seconds on a first-down clock.

    The play-caller might say this to get it started:

    "I had already decided to throw if I got this first down."

- Then, he quickly calls the formation and the pass and thinks beyond and out loud while the ref gets the ball ready for play.

    "If I get a first down, I throw again. No first down, and no stopped clock, I call time-out. Close to the 23 or beyond, I will have a first down and will run."

- You complete your pass for a first down on the 21. 00:27 shows. The play-caller calls the run that he had decided to call if he got close to the 23. Again, he thinks beyond and out loud.

    "First down or out-of-bounds, I run again. No stopped clock, I call time-out."

- You run. Plus 11. First down at 00:20. He quickly calls the run and, again, thinks out loud:

    "First-and-goal. Clock stops after this, I run again. Clock doesn't stop, I call time-out."

- You run. Plus three. The clock does not stop. You call time-out. It is 2nd-and-goal on the seven, with 00:13 seconds and one time-out remaining.

    To your QB you say, "Let's run off-tackle to put the ball in front of the goalposts, then call the time-out. Tell Alex to stay in the middle and not to zig and zag."

- You execute the run, and the QB calls time-out. You kick and win.

This is so difficult to do that you want a play-caller in training to have all the time he needs to practice thinking out loud—a whole minute each time if necessary. Very gradually, then, you can constrict the time until it is down to a few seconds.

About the Author

Homer Smith is a former football coach with 40 years of experience, including 38 years teaching quarterbacks. During his illustrious career, he received numerous honors, including being named District Three Coach of the Year (1969), Eastern Coach of the Year (1977), and *Sporting News* Offensive Coach of the Year (1984). In 1997, his final year of coaching, Smith was a finalist for the Broyles (Assistant Coach of the Year) Award, and in 2006 he was the recipient of the American Football Coaches Association Outstanding Achievement Award. He holds degrees from Princeton, Stanford, and Harvard. Retired, Smith lives in Tuscaloosa, Alabama with his wife, Kathy.